Entrepreneurs Who Built India

ALSO IN THIS SERIES

Gujarmal Modi: The Resolute Industrialist (2022)
Lala Shri Ram: The Man Who Saw Tomorrow (2023)

Entrepreneurs Who Built India
Ramkrishna Dalmia
THE FEARLESS RISK-TAKER

SONU BHASIN

HARPER
BUSINESS

First published in India by Harper Business 2025
An imprint of HarperCollins *Publishers*
HarperCollins *Publishers* India, Cyber City,
Building 10-A, Gurugram, Haryana – 122002, India
www.harpercollins.co.in

2 4 6 8 10 9 7 5 3 1

Copyright © Sonu Bhasin 2025

P-ISBN: 978-93-6989-777-3
E-ISBN: 978-93-6989-968-5

The views and opinions expressed in this book are the author's own
and the facts are as reported by her, and the publishers are not
in any way liable for the same.

Sonu Bhasin asserts the moral right
to be identified as the author of this work.

All rights reserved. No part of this publication may be reproduced,
stored in a retrieval system, or transmitted, in any form or by any means,
electronic, mechanical, photocopying, recording or otherwise,
without the prior permission of the publishers.

Without limiting the exclusive rights of any author, contributor or the publisher
of this publication, any unauthorized use of this publication to train generative
artificial intelligence (AI) technologies is expressly prohibited. HarperCollins
also exercise their rights under Article 4(3) of the Digital Single Market
Directive 2019/790 and expressly reserve this publication from the text and
data-mining exception.

Typeset in 11.5/15.5 Warnock Pro
by HarperCollins *Publishers* India Pvt. Ltd

Printed and bound at
Thomson Press (India) Ltd

This book is produced from independently certified FSC® paper
to ensure responsible forest management.

HarperCollins *Publishers*, Macken House, 39/40 Mayor Street Upper,
Dublin 1, D01 C9W8, Ireland

To the two men in my life—Juggi and Karan. You guys are my anchors in the choppy seas of life.

Contents

Introduction ix

1. The Story of Ramkrishna's Family 1
2. Growing Up in Chirawa and Calcutta 10
3. Ramkrishna Gets Married and Runs Away from Home 19
4. Ramkrishna Is Bitten by the Speculation Bug 31
5. Lady Luck Finally Smiles on Ramkrishna 42
6. Speculating in Silver and Becoming Wealthy 68
7. Ramkrishna's Guru and Mentor—Baldev Das Nathani 83
8. Ramkrishna's Brother Jaidayal Grows Up 107
9. The Apple of Ramkrishna's Eye—His Daughter Rama 116
10. Baby Steps—From Speculator to Industrialist 121
11. Ramkrishna Takes on the Mighty ACC 141

Contents

12.	Ramkrishna Buys *Times of India* Newspaper	172
13.	Family Life and the Quest for a Son	186
14.	Ramkrishna's Deep Friendship with Jinnah	206
15.	Division of the Dalmia-Jain Group	220
16.	Ramkrishna Is Sent to Jail	229
17.	Illness Takes a Toll on Ramkrishna	242
	About the Series: Entrepreneurs Who Built India	248
	Acknowledgements	253
	References	255

Introduction

IT is perhaps a sad reflection of our times that the name of Ramkrishna Dalmia is synonymous with his six wives rather than as the founder of the third-largest business group of Undivided India. It was only the Tatas and the Birlas that were ahead of the Dalmia-Jain Group in the 1940s.

Ramkrishna's foray into the business world started with a modest job with his maternal uncle who was a bullion trader in the Calcutta market. From there, Ramkrishna went on to build one of the most diversified businesses in Undivided India—from sugar to cement; from banks to insurance companies; from aviation to cargo; from biscuits to dairy products; from newspapers to glass; from paper to oil—these are just some examples of the diversity. Dalmianagar—one of the largest industrial townships in India, located in the Rohtas district of Bihar, was named after Ramkrishna Dalmia. Having inducted his son-in-law, Shanti Prasad Jain, into the business, Ramkrishna formed the Dalmia Jain Group, which was a formidable business group of its time.

The decline started just before Independence when the three partners—Ramkrishna Dalmia, his brother Jaidayal Dalmia and his son-in-law Shanti Prasad Jain—decided to split the business. While some individual businesses and companies went on to do well, the might of the Dalmia-Jain group diminished.

Ramkrishna Dalmia and the Dalmia-Jain Group are not a lone example of a thriving business empire set up in pre-Independence India, growing in stature and size in the following years and then losing their way as they were hit either by family feuds or liberalization or both. The Indian industrial and corporate sector is scattered with people and businesses that had seen their glory in the days that some consider to be the most challenging in the lives of Indian businessmen—the years between 1947 and 1991.

India became independent in 1947, and the newfound freedom brought forth aspirations and dreams not just for individual people but also collective dreams of social, political and economic freedom. However, the first prime minister envisaged a developmental model that had the state playing a dominant role as an entrepreneur as well as the funder of private businesses. The dreams of the economic freedom that entrepreneurs had of the new India quickly withered away as the British Raj was quickly replaced by the Licence Raj.

Due to the restrictions placed by the Licence Raj, which many say was a complex and opaque system, being an entrepreneur in India meant a big headache. Further, the entrepreneurial spirit was kept in tight leash by the complex and authoritative system. Entrepreneurs were successful not so much because of what they did but because of who they knew. Such was the dependence on the benign hand of the government that businessmen, due to their association with the politician and bureaucrat, also were enveloped in the cloud of corruption in the minds of the general public.

However, people forget that there were many entrepreneurs, and indeed businesses, during those particularly challenging times that worked tirelessly to make the new India. Ramkrishna Dalmia was one of them. It certainly was not easy, but he persevered.

During the British rule, Ramkrishna Dalmia, like any other entrepreneur of that time, faced problems around transport, logistics, communication and even skilled talent. Most transport of material and supplies was on slow-moving carts or using the very few motor vehicles available. Getting in touch with mills and factories in remote locations was tough. Most machinery had to be imported and then it was a challenge to find the workers to run the machinery. There were no MBA institutes to churn out batches of management students who could run businesses; most entrepreneurs relied on family members to run the various businesses.

As India became independent, some of these challenges remained and some new ones were added. The new challenges primarily revolved around the new 'system' of doing business in independent India. True, Ramkrishna Dalmia did learn how to 'manage' the system, but it did require entrepreneurial skills to set up new businesses, and manage and grow existing ones within the tight framework of the system. Manufacturing is never an easy business, and the Licence Raj made achieving economies of scale even more difficult with the restrictions on the numbers that could be produced. It is to the credit of Ramkrishna Dalmia that he not only went about his work diligently, but also created products that became household names at that time. Unfortunately, most of those are present today in a diluted manner or are almost forgotten.

However, what cannot and should not be forgotten is Ramkrishna's contribution in being part of a group of entrepreneurs who worked to lay down the foundation of Indian economy and industry. If it were not for him and other stalwarts who worked against the odds and set up businesses, provided employment to many people and kept the Indian economy growing, India of today would not be where she is currently.

Thus, it is important to bring these entrepreneurs out of their obscurity and present to the new generation as the entrepreneurs who built India.

This is the story of Ramkrishna Dalmia, the man who came from nowhere and became the third richest industrialist in Undivided India.

Ramkrishna's life is a remarkable story of ambition, resilience and unparalleled business acumen. Born in Chirawa in Rajasthan, Ramkrishna's journey from poverty to becoming one of India's most influential industrialists is nothing short of inspirational. Further, his story is not just one of financial success but also of immense contribution to the nation's development.

Ramkrishna's early life was marked by hardship as he moved to Calcutta with his family in search of better opportunities. At the tender age of eighteen, the responsibility of supporting his family fell upon him after the death of his father.

In the early twentieth century, first working with his maternal uncle and then on his own, Ramkrishna entered the world of

Introduction

bullion speculation, focusing primarily on silver. During the 1910s and 1920s, silver prices were volatile and Ramkrishna capitalized on these market swings with remarkable precision. Destiny seemed to play an important role in Ramkrishna's early success, particularly in his silver speculation. A pivotal moment came when he made a fortuitous bet on rising silver prices, just as the global demand surged. This was a turning point that transformed his financial status.

His aggressive and bold speculative bets resulted in substantial profits. There were some losses as well, no doubt, as no speculator can have a continuous winning streak. However, unlike other contemporaries who hesitated in volatile markets, Ramkrishna thrived on uncertainty and made crores by correctly anticipating price movements. He had no formal training but worked with a natural flair for risk-taking. This flair, along with his sharp instincts, yielded extraordinary profits.

However, Ramkrishna's ambitions extended beyond the unpredictable world of speculation. With the wealth he amassed, Ramkrishna began investing in industrial enterprises, transitioning from a speculator to a long-term industrialist. This transition was also fuelled by his deep desire for respect from others, which seemed to elude him in his avatar as a speculator.

In the 1930s, he founded Dalmianagar in Bihar—an industrial township that housed large-scale operations in sugar, cement, paper and chemicals. This signalled his commitment to building tangible, lasting assets that could sustain his fortune beyond the highs and lows of speculation. By the 1940s, Ramkrishna had become one of India's most powerful business figures, diversifying his holdings across multiple industries. His most famous acquisition came in 1946 when he purchased *The Times of India* in a bold move that startled the British establishment. He used the influence of the press to extend both his business and political reach. The newspaper provided him a platform to voice his strong political opinions, which very often put him at odds with prominent political figures including the then prime minister, Jawaharlal Nehru. This foray in the media world proved costly for Ramkrishna, highlighting the inherent risks of mixing business with politics.

Ramkrishna's legacy is often overshadowed by the towering industrialists who came after him, yet his impact on India's business landscape was profound. Despite his financial success, Ramkrishna faced numerous challenges and controversies that obscured his contributions to India's industrial landscape. Behind the headlines lay a man driven by restless ambition and an unyielding belief in his destiny. Ramkrishna often attributed his early successes to a sense of divine guidance, believing that destiny had chosen him for greater things. This total belief in his preordained success fuelled his confidence, allowing him to take ever-larger risks and eventually transition from a speculative trader to India's third-largest industrialist.

The public image of Ramkrishna is that of a ruthless businessman who played the game of power with unmatched cunning. But there is a lesser-known side to his personality. Ramkrishna was a deeply religious man who funded temples and spiritual initiatives, blending his material pursuits with a profound sense of faith. He was also a patron of arts, supporting cultural endeavours that sought to revive India's heritage. Despite his tough exterior, Ramkrishna was a man intensely loyal and capable of great generosity.

Ramkrishna was a man of startling contradictions. He was a devout Hindu who championed traditional, almost orthodox, values, yet was an audacious entrepreneur who thrived on disruption. He was a fiery nationalist who was passionate about Swadeshi ideals yet was a shrewd capitalist who expanded his business empire using modern, and often street-smart, tactics. He was a patriarch who sought to uphold family name and honour, yet his own personal life was market by unconventional choices and public controversies. To understand Ramkrishna is to grapple with these contradictions—and to appreciate how they fuelled his rise as one of India's most enigmatic business magnates.

One particular contradiction was Ramkrishna's friendship with Muhammed Ali Jinnah. They shared an unexpected yet deep friendship that transcended their stark personal differences. Jinnah had studied in Britain, was a lawyer and the leader of the Muslim League. He was known for his love for a good non-vegetarian diet, appreciation for cigars and drinks. He led a Western lifestyle. Ramkrishna, on the other hand, was a devout Hindu industrialist, a complete vegetarian, abstained from alcohol and maintained traditional practices.

The contradictions in Ramkrishna's life eventually led to his fall from grace. His aggressive business practices, along with his personal controversies, brought him into conflict with the newly independent State. In 1956, Ramkrishna was convicted of financial impropriety and imprisoned some years later—a stunning reversal for a man who once seemed invincible.

It is sad that the business empire lost its position as the third-largest industrial group after the three-way split between the brothers and Ramkrishna's son-in-law. And then Ramkrishna's own share of the business suffered due to the many legal cases on the one hand, and his own ill health on the other. The fact that he had a total of eighteen children from his four wives (two of his six wives did not bear any children), six of which were sons, did not help matters when it came to passing on the businesses to the next generation.

Notwithstanding this, the story of Ramkrishna is instructive even for the entrepreneurs of today who often complain about the many constraints they face in setting up and then running their enterprises. As I travelled back in time with Ramkrishna—the speculator and then the industrialist—it was evident that he looked at constraints not as roadblocks but as minor speed-breakers. The modern-day entrepreneur could also learn from Ramkrishna the art of focusing on people, especially workers, along with a strict focus on discipline and family values. But mostly the entrepreneurs of today would find, as they read the story of Ramkrishna, that hard work, determination, grit and focus go hand in hand with the spirit of entrepreneurship.

As you read the story in the following pages, you will find that my role as the author is that of a narrator. I have taken creative licence when recounting the stories of various people, their conversations, including those of Ramkrishna himself. Most dialogue is imagined though all the situations are real. Some of the names used in the story are fictitious. Many of the people in the story are no longer alive and thus, the narration is based on the memories of other people and/or the archival material shared by a few sons and daughter of Ramkrishna. The creative licence has been used with the objective of bringing alive the times gone by and the man who was Ramkrishna.

Now presenting to you Ramkrishna Dalmia—one of the entrepreneurs who built India. His life exemplifies how entrepreneurial vision, combined with the strategic use of speculative gains, can transform personal wealth into a business empire that shapes a nation's industrial future.

1

The Story of Ramkrishna's Family

RAMKRISHNA Dalmia was born in Chirawa on 7 April 1893. While Chirawa may be a name unfamiliar to many, the families and individuals from this small town have gone on to gain name, recognition and fame in both India and across the world.

Chirawa is a small municipal town and a tehsil in the Jhunjhunu district of Rajasthan. It sits in the Shekhawati region of the state and lies approximately 200 km south-west of Delhi. It is said to be over 500 years old. Chirawa has also been known as one of the richest tehsils in the region. At the start of the twentieth century, it boasted of approximately 125 'lakhpati' businessmen.

Ramkrishna's family could trace its history in Chirawa for five generations before him. The earliest mention of a Dalmia in Chirawa is of Kaniram Dalmia. He moved to Chirawa from

Sohansara in present-day Haryana around 1783, a little over one hundred years before Ramkrishna was born.

Ramkrishna's great-grandfather, Kashi Ram Dalmia, was a wealthy businessman. His early years were spent in Bhiwani, a city in modern-day Haryana.

Kashi Ram was of small build and dark complexion. He was a devout Hindu and practised deep philanthropy. He built a temple in Bhiwani, which was popularly known as Kashi Ramji ka Mandir.

Kashi Ram's day would begin early. He would wake up at 4 a.m. every day. In the absence of a free-flowing river, Kashi Ram would go to a well for his morning bath. Not only would he bathe at that early hour himself, while it was still dark, but he also ensured that his cook did the same. The cook was a Vaishnav Brahmin, and Kashi Ram insisted that his food be cooked only after the cook had cleansed himself.

The morning cleansing ritual was followed by prayers. Kashi Ram would spend many hours, almost till midday, in his prayers. He would start by the *jap* (recitation) of the Gayatri Mantra, followed by the jap of Ram Naam, which he would recite one lakh times.

Kashi Ram's wife, Amri Devi, followed in her husband's footsteps. She too would recite the Ram Naam, and even surpassed her husband—reciting it one lakh and twenty-five thousand times each day. The couple's children were also brought up with these values. They saw their father live the Sanatani life and imbibed it unconsciously.

The story of Kashi Ram's charity was well-known in the area. After his morning puja, Kashi Ram would distribute food to all who came to the temple that he had built. It was only after they had been given food that Kashi Ram would eat his own meal. The temple also organized sermons and bhajans after the daily prayers. The head pujari would ring the temple bell as a signal that the prayers were to begin. The ringing of the bell would be accompanied by the beating of drums. These sounds could be heard across the village. The local residents would start trickling into the temple premises once they heard the bells and the drums. While some people came to join in the prayers, many came for the free food.

The food-seekers would line up in an orderly manner outside the temple kitchen. Kashi Ram would go there after his morning prayers. As he walked along the queue of waiting people, making his way to the front, he would acknowledge the people's greetings. Some wished him Ram-Ram while others folded their hands and bowed. Others stepped out of the line and bent down to touch his feet. Kashi Ram acknowledged each greeting with folded hands and a mild smile.

Once he reached the front of the line, the cooks would bring out a thali of food they had cooked. Kashi Ram would taste it to check if the salt and other ingredients were fine. Only after he had declared the food fit for eating would the cooks start ladling it out to the waiting people.

After this tasting, Kashi Ram would eat his own meal. After that, he would go to his shop. He was a wealthy trader, and the size of his shop reflected his success. It was a large shop with many attendants. As he was a well-known and much-liked person, his shop was never short of customers.

Kashi Ram's charity continued at the shop. Anyone who came to him with a request would be given what they needed. In spite of his orthodox beliefs, he did not differentiate on the basis of caste or religion when it came to charity. People would come to ask him for all kinds of things—clothes, sugar, ghee, cooking vessels, vegetables, grinding machines, and even needle and thread. Kashi Ram ensured that every person was given what they needed.

In those days, Rajasthan had a custom of donating to Brahmin households. To this end, the *Panch* of every village had a list of all Brahmin households in the village.

The *Panch* maintained two lists—the *Navan* and the *Thali*. The *Navan* list was known as the people's list or the name list and listed all the Brahmins in the village. Whenever a child was born into a Brahmin house, their name would be added to this list. Similarly, whenever there was a death in a Brahmin family, the name of the deceased would be removed from the list.

The *Thali* list kept a record of the number of people in each household. This was important because a Brahmin household with more than five members was eligible to receive donations. Donations were not given to individual members but to the household as a unit.

When residents of a village left to go to bigger towns for better livelihood opportunities, they would often send donations to the *Panch* for the village, and he would distribute this money in accordance with the lists maintained by him.

Kashi Ram also donated to the Brahmin households and was one of the most generous contributors in the area.

He lived a long life, reaching the age of eighty-five. Throughout his years, and especially during the later stages of his life, he donated generously to charity. Although he had been a philanthropist all his life, as he grew older his charity increased. He believed that by giving away all his material assets and money he would have a better afterlife. So, he started giving away everything, little by little, until almost nothing remained.

In his final years, he lived more like an ascetic than as a wealthy trader.

While he may have ensured a better afterlife for himself, Kashi Ram's children and grandchildren were forced to live a life of poverty after his death.

Kashi Ram's son Shriram was Ramkrishna's grandfather. He had seen and lived the good life in his early years. When his father began giving away all his wealth and assets Shriram could do nothing but look on as a mute spectator. Children in the nineteenth century did not interfere in their parents' decisions.

As a result of his father's charity, Shriram did not have the luxury of living the good life. With no assets or income to his name, he was forced to work for other people. He was married to Narayani Devi, who belonged to a reputed and wealthy family from Churu. The marriage had taken place when Kashi Ram was still wealthy. Narayani Devi was short in height but had a strong personality. Shriram and Narayani Devi's son, Harjimal, was Ramkrishna's father.

Harjimal had heard stories about Kashi Ram from his father. He, in turn, related those stories to Ramkrishna. Even though Harjimal was poor, he wanted his son to be aware and proud of his legacy.

'It may be true, son, that we have no money now. But you must remember your legacy. Your great-grandfather and his forefathers were wealthy traders and businessmen. The entire village respected them,' Harjimal told Ramkrishna as the two sat together eating breakfast. Ramkrishna, who had an inquisitive mind, wanted to know more.

'But Bapu, if great-grandfather was wealthy, why are we poor? Is that why no one respects us? Because we don't have money?' he asked innocently. He had seen how wealthy people in the village were treated by others. He also saw and felt how his own family was treated. Even as a young child he felt that although they were not mistreated, he and his family deserved more.

'Son, this is the way of life. When you become older you will realize that no matter how good or helpful you are, it is always people with money who are respected,' Harjimal responded with a deep sigh. He had not lived a life of plenty. But he, in turn, had heard from his father about the wealthy but simple lifestyle of Kashi Ram. He sighed softly again as he wished for a better future for his son.

'I will remember that, Bapu, for sure,' promised Ramkrishna as he started to get up. But then a thought struck him. He sat right back down.

'Bapu, did my grandfather also have to go through this kind of treatment? Surely people would have remembered my great-grandfather and would have accorded him the same respect, no?' asked Ramkrishna with wide-eyed curiosity.

'Let me tell you what happened with my father—your grandfather, Shriramji. He lived a life of luxury while his father was alive. But even when he was alive, your great-grandfather had already started giving away most of his wealth,' Harjimal said, as he burped softly.

He had finished his breakfast and knew he should leave for work. But he also wanted Ramkrishna to learn about his family legacy. He believed it was important for the child to know his past. Harjimal was trying to light a fire in Ramkrishna—the fire to reclaim the old glory of the Dalmia family.

'It must have been hard for grandfather, Bapu,' Ramkrishna said matter-of-factly. His comment shook Harjimal out of his reverie as he had been dreaming about a better future for his son.

'Yes, you are right, son. It was difficult. He was forced to look for work so he could support his family after his father's death. His brother-in-law gave him a job. His sister was married into a well-to-do household, as the marriage had taken place when the family was still wealthy. Your grandfather's brother-in-law appointed him as a *munim*—an accountant and manager of cash,' explained Harjimal as he leaned forward to straighten his son's kurta—it had been falling off his small shoulders.

'It would have been easy for grandfather to do that job, Bapu. Look at how good we all are with numbers,' said Ramkrishna proudly but with a grimace as he shrugged off his father's effort to groom him.

Harjimal smiled.

'Yes, it was easy. But then one day some cash went missing from the safe. When he discovered this, your grandfather immediately told his brother-in-law about it. Not surprisingly, he suspected your grandfather and accused him to his face.'

'But why would someone do that?' Ramkrishna exclaimed. 'Did they not see how grandfather had looked after all the cash in his custody? Why would he steal, and that too from the safe box?' asked young Ramkrishna, not understanding the logic of it all.

'Son, this is the way of the world, unfortunately. Poor people are often unfairly judged as being unethical. Your grandfather was poor, and so he was suspected,' said Harjimal sadly.

'How did my grandfather react? I hope he left the job,' Ramkrishna was affronted.

'Had he left the job immediately, people would have assumed that he was indeed the culprit. So, he gritted his teeth and stayed on. He also knew that no matter how much he denied it, he would not be believed,' Harjimal continued.

'So, what did he do?' Ramkrishna sat on the ground cross-legged, his hands under his chin. He looked at his father expectantly as he waited for him to speak.

'There was no postal system in those days. So, your grandfather sent a messenger to his wife—your grandmother. He asked her to send all her jewellery through the messenger,' Harjimal said.

'And did Dadi do that?' Ramkrishna was very curious. He knew how fond women were of their ornaments. He wanted to know if his grandmother had parted with her jewellery easily.

'Of course she did, Ramkrishna. She sent her jewellery after the messenger told her why Shriram needed it. As soon as he received the jewels, he sold them and got the money for it. But before he could give the money to his brother-in-law, the local purohit spoke with him.' Harjimal had forgotten about going to work. He was keen on finishing the story.

'Why? Did the purohit know something? Did God tell the purohit who the thief was?' asked Ramkrishna innocently but with excitement.

'Yes, in a way. Yes. This purohit had overheard a local potter telling his wife to stuff all the money in their mattress and leave immediately before anyone realized that they had left. The purohit confronted the potter, who confessed that it was the brother-in-law's cook who had stolen the money and had given it to the potter for safekeeping. The potter, in turn, wanted to take the money and run away,' Harjimal told the story with a wry smile.

'So, was the cook caught?' asked Ramkrishna as he leaned forward, his eyes shining in anticipation.

'Of course, the cook was caught,' said Harjimal, waving his hand about.

'And then what did grandfather do?' wondered Ramkrishna, almost asking the question to himself.

'Your grandfather had been very hurt by the accusations. He felt humiliated. His respect had been trampled upon. He left the employment of his brother-in-law,' said Harjimal.

'They must've been sorry to lose the services of grandfather,' Ramkrishna said shrewdly.

'Of course, they certainly were. They pleaded with him to stay on. But your grandfather was adamant. He may have been poor, but he had his self-respect. He knew that he came from a family of repute. He knew that his brother-in-law had also benefitted from his father's large-heartedness and charity. Thus, the accusation was twice as hurtful for him. He left,' said Harjimal as he too got up to leave. He adjusted his dhoti and smoothened his kurta with his hands in preparation to go out.

'Bapu, when I grow up, I will earn a lot of money and will get a lot of respect,' said Ramkrishna with a determined look on his face as he looked up at his father, who has stood up by now.

Harjimal smiled, bent down and ruffled his son's hair affectionately.

'Son, you are destined for big things in life. You will go far, believe me. But remember one thing: no matter how rich you become, always be mindful of the dignity of the poor. Just because they don't have money does not mean that they don't deserve respect,' said Harjimal.

These words stayed with Ramkrishna throughout his life.

2

Growing Up in Chirawa and Calcutta

RAMKRISHNA grew up in a humble household. His parents, Harjimal and Jadiya Devi Dalmia, were deeply religious. They were materially poor but spiritually rich. Harjimal earned about Rs 75 per month, within which he had to support a full household that comprised three generations—his mother, his wife and his five children.

Ramkrishna had three sisters—two older than him and one younger. He also had a younger brother. His two elder sisters were named Manibai and Basantibai. Ramkrishna was closer to his younger siblings. His younger sister, Godavari, was his playmate for many years till the youngest child of the family, a son, came along. Jaidayal was eleven years younger than Ramkrishna. As Ramkrishna himself had a child not long after Jaidayal was born, he treated his brother more like a son than a sibling all through his life.

Growing up in a household that was not wealthy was not easy, but nor was it difficult. Harjimal worked as the head *munim* in a firm called Kirana Baira Bux Bagle, which imported almonds and raisins from Rangoon, Burma (now Myanmar). The work was hard, and Harjimal was not very happy as it was menial work and required no application of the mind. When he got an opportunity to work with his brother-in-law (his wife's brother) in Calcutta, he took it up eagerly, even though his wife was not happy. Jadiya Devi was of the firm belief that working with relatives led to unhappy results. Even Harjimal's mother cautioned him against working for a relative.

'Remember what happened with your father, Harjimal. And now you are making the same mistake,' warned Narayani Devi as she tried to get her son to change his mind.

'You are right, Mother. But I have to look after the family. And there are no jobs here. Jadiya's brother has offered me a job. I must accept so I can earn money,' Harjimal explained patiently.

'Promise me, son, that you will maintain your dignity. Do not allow anyone to treat you badly just because you don't have as much money as them,' said Narayani Devi.

'I promise, Mother. My dignity and self-respect are important to me,' Harjimal reassured her as he bent to touch her feet.

Ramkrishna, witnessing this exchange, resolved to earn money as soon as he could. He knew that his family was poor. He also knew that his great-grandfather had been a man of wealth. The stories he had heard made him realize that the world had treated his grandfather very differently from how it was treating him and his family.

Ramkrishna was not a particularly handsome child. He was wheatish in colour and he was not very tall. He had inherited these physical traits from his great-grandfather. He had also inherited a head for numbers from his grandfather along with a sharp, intelligent mind. Though Ramkrishna sometimes wished he looked different, he would quickly remind himself that Kashi Ram had been a wealthy man, a man who had commanded respect. He told himself that he was fortunate to resemble his great-grandfather. He resolved to never let his looks and height come in the way of his ambition.

'My great-grandfather was a rich man, and I too will be like him. And I am not going to give away my wealth in charity,' Ramkrishna told his mother one day while he was having lunch. As his father had gone to Calcutta to work for his brother-in-law, Ramkrishna was the eldest man in the house. Even though still a child, he felt responsible for the family.

'What will you do, beta? You know we don't have a family business. We also don't have any money for setting up a business. How will you earn money?' asked Jadiya Devi as she wiped the remnants of food from her son's face.

'Mother, you know that the power of the mind is everything. Even our shastras teach us that the mind is the most powerful part of our body. I will make sure that I develop my mind and use it to earn money. Then you will see—we will all be respected, and no one will treat us like nobodies,' vowed Ramkrishna seriously.

'Beta, you have a sunny disposition. You make friends easily. Everyone likes you. They all like talking to you. Remember that ultimately, it is the people who matter. I have no doubt that you will earn money. But always remember to treat people well,' Jadiya Devi gave some unsolicited advice to her son.

'Mother, Father also told me the same thing. I understand and will remember this,' said Ramkrishna as he rose from the floor.

Even as a child, Ramkrishna was different from other children. He was not interested in playing with the other children. He started school at the age of five and soon demonstrated his excellent grasp of numbers. Within four years, by the age of nine, he had learnt all that his teacher, Jhabarmalji, had to teach him. He then looked to another teacher, Devkinandanji, to teach him English. He also learnt Urdu. He learnt by rote the basics of the language—alif, be, pe, te, and the rest of the alphabet. His rudimentary knowledge of English and Urdu, which he developed further later in Calcutta, helped Ramkrishna throughout his life.

However, it was his knowledge of Marwari, mathematics and the Mudiya script that helped Ramkrishna in his business endeavours. In those days, business accounts were maintained in Mudiya. Also known as the *Mahajani* or bankers' script, Mudiya was a Brahmi-based writing system that was used in northern India until the mid-twentieth century. It was employed for maintaining financial records and accounts. Students, especially those from the trading community, learnt the script as it helped them in their businesses.

Even though Ramkrishna was not a businessman, he invested time in learning Mudiya as he was sure that, even if not in his own business, it would help him in finding a job.

Ramkrishna revered his father. There was no other male role model whom he could look up to. He was fascinated by the stories of Kashi Ram, his wealth and his charitable activities. He would sit with his father whenever possible, asking him to share more about his great-grandfather.

'Bapu, how did great-grandfather earn all that money?' asked Ramkrishna one evening when his father was home.

'Beta, his father had the same business. Your great-grandfather simply carried it forward,' replied Harjimal wistfully, gazing into the distance. It was as if he were wishing that he, too, had inherited a business from his father to carry forward.

'Bapu, you told me that people used to touch his feet wherever he went. Is that true?' Ramkrishna had a bagful of questions. He was enamoured by his great-grandfather and wanted to know everything possible about him.

'Yes, son. Your great-grandfather, my grandfather, was a much-respected man. People of his village loved him as well. He did a lot for them. They respected him and touched his feet as a mark of this respect. They also did it because they wanted his *ashirwaad*, his blessings, so that they, too, could become as rich as him,' explained Harjimal.

'Bapu, did people respect and love him because he was rich?' Ramkrishna was curious whether there was a simple corelation between wealth and respect.

'Son, remember that riches and wealth don't always translate into respect and respectability. Riches can be acquired by unfair means as well. A dacoit may be rich, but is he respected? Tell me,' Harjimal had a question of his own.

Ramkrishna had been listening intently to his father. As he was asked the question, he shook his head in response.

'So, beta, even you agree that a dacoit is not respected. People may fear him, but they certainly don't respect him. So, being rich and powerful is not enough. What is important is that you have to earn money the right way. And you must also use the money not only for yourself but also for others,' Harjimal counselled.

'Bapu, what you are saying is true. But using the money for others? Isn't that what great-grandfather did? And look where it has landed us. We are poor and no one touches our feet,' Ramkrishna said plaintively.

'Beta, you read the shastras, don't you? What do they teach us? They teach us that the life we are living is the result of our karmas carried over from our past lives. Perhaps my grandfather had to pay some debts from an earlier life. So, he gave away his wealth. In a sense, he cleansed himself of all past misdeeds and ensured that his afterlife would be a good one,' explained Harjimal. He knew that Ramkrishna had some knowledge of the shastras and also that the child was keen on knowing more about spiritual development and, therefore, would understand this.

'So, Bapu, why are we living like this? Are we paying some debts from our past life?' wondered Ramkrishna.

'Beta, maybe you are being given a chance to cleanse your soul and your karma in this life. Who knows what karma you are carrying from your past lives. Instead of focusing on the here and now, focus on the future. Just because we are poor now does not mean we will always be poor,' Harjimal said optimistically. He wanted his son to believe that he could do better in life.

'That is true, Bapu. I will work hard to earn money and be rich,' Ramkrishna jumped up in excitement.

'That is a good thought, son. But remember, as I have already told you, do not harm anyone in your quest to earn money, and also use the money for the good of others,' cautioned the older man.

'Of course, Bapu. But I will not give away everything for sure! In that way I will be different from my great-grandfather.

I will give to the needy, of course,' said Ramkrishna with a chuckle.

'It will happen, son, it will happen. You are a bright child. You will go far. Just remember to work hard and treat everyone with respect. You cannot hope to get respect if you don't give it to others in the first place,' Harjimal said softly but firmly. He wanted his son to understand that money alone did not bring respect; it was how one treated others that truly earned it.

Ramkrishna listened attentively and absorbed the advice given by his father. He looked up to Harjimal and aspired to emulate him. Harjimal was a stoic man who never lost his temper and always maintained his equilibrium. As a child, Ramkrishna made many mistakes, but all Harjimal would say was, 'Do not repeat these mistakes, son.'

Ramkrishna's faith in religion and spirituality began at an early age. He observed his father follow a daily routine that included several religious activities. His father's day would begin early with a dip in the river. The *sandhya kala* would be performed thrice a day—in the morning before sunrise, at midday and in the evening before sunset.

'Sandhya kala' is derived from Sanskrit, with 'san' meaning good, 'dhya' meaning to meditate and 'kala' meaning time. It refers to the best times of the day for meditation. The sandhya kalas, practised at three different times of the day, have different names. *Brahma muhurta sandhya* is performed before sunrise when the mind is calm, and the distractions of the day have not yet begun. The next is *Vishnu sandhya*, which marks the time to take a break from the daily routine to refresh and refocus the mind. The last one, *Mahesha sandhya*, eases the transition from work to winding down for the day.

Every Sunday, Harjimal would recite *Adityahriday*, or the prayer of the Sun God, and involve his elder son in some of his religious practices. As a result, Ramkrishna grew up with a deep faith in religion. He scrupulously observed the tenets of the Vaishnavas, applying them to all aspects of his life. Following the scriptures faithfully made him somewhat detached from the material world, but this did not diminish his ambition or desire for wealth. He always remembered his great-grandfather, who was rich but lived a simple life, and was so detached that he gave away all his material possessions before his death.

While Harjimal was in Calcutta working with his brother-in-law, his family had remained in Chirawa. However, when a plague broke out in India in 1904, Ramkrishna's mother and grandmother took the family to Malsisar, a small town about 40 km from Chirawa. Ramkrishna's grandmother came from Malsisar, and her father was a wealthy man with a big house. She wanted the family to live in comfort, especially as Jadiya Devi was pregnant.

On 11 December 1904, Jadiya Devi gave birth to her second son. Ramkrishna was very excited. Having been surrounded by women—his sisters, mother and grandmother—he was delighted that there was finally another boy in the family. Harjimal, who was in Calcutta, did not know about the birth of his second son. There were no telephones, and the ordinary post would take a couple of days. So Ramkrishna decided to send a telegram to his father. At the post office, he discovered that the cost of a telegram depended on the number of words in the message. Ramkrishna wrote a short message, sending it almost for free. He simply wrote 'son born'.

The younger son was named Jaidayal. The newborn baby was eleven years younger than Ramkrishna. Due to the large age gap, Ramkrishna had a paternal attitude towards Jaidayal right from the start.

After the birth of Jaidayal, the family returned to Chirawa. However, Ramkrishna went to Calcutta to spend some time with his father. Harjimal had leased a small room in a building owned by a distant relative. Even though it was small, Harjimal paid a rent of Rs 8 per month for the room. The building owner, Prahladrai Dalmia, had two sons who were a little older than Ramkrishna. Prahladrai had engaged a private tutor for his sons, who came every day to teach them. Ramkrishna wanted to join the lessons with the two boys, but Harjimal could not afford to pay the tuition fees of Rs 2 per month.

Ramkrishna was very keen to educate himself. He was convinced that the path to wealth lay in gaining education and knowledge. But he was also aware that the tutor cost money, which he did not have.

Ramkrishna found a solution to the problem. The tutor would teach his two students in a room on the first floor. Ramkrishna would sit just outside the room and listen to all the lessons. He had a sharp mind and was able to grasp the lessons better than his two cousins. Impressed by the young lad, the tutor told Harjimal that his young son was very clever and would go far in life.

3

Ramkrishna Gets Married and Runs Away from Home

HARJIMAL continued to support his family back in Chirawa with his meagre means. He was even able to marry off his three daughters, which was an important milestone for a householder in those days. He also got his eldest son, Ramkrishna, married before his own death.

As was the practice in the early twentieth century, Ramkrishna got married young—at the age of eleven. His first wife, Narbada, was almost twelve years old at the time of the wedding. She was handsome, with a wheatish complexion and sweet voice. The match had been suggested by Ramkrishna's eldest sister's father-in-law.

The wedding was held in Chirawa. Harjimal, who was working in Calcutta, returned to the village for the occasion.

The ceremonies took place in the evening—at *godhuli*. Godhuli refers to the time of day when the cows return home from the pastures. As the herds move, they kick up dust from the ground, giving this time of day its name.

Even though it was his own son's wedding, Harjimal did not neglect his daily routine of religious observances. After the *varmala* ceremony, Harjimal went off to do the sandhya kala. He told no one and slipped out of the wedding venue unnoticed.

When it was time for the *pheras*, people began looking for Harjimal but could not find him anywhere. The house was not large enough for someone to get lost in. The guests, puzzled by the absence of the groom's father, started talking among themselves.

'Arrey, where has the father of the bridegroom disappeared?' said one person as he sat with a group of men.

'Harjimalji was here a while back. Who knows where he has gone,' wondered another, almost talking to himself.

'How will the pheras take place without the father? I hope he knows about the muhurat,' fretted another.

Someone from Chirawa, who was familiar with Harjimal's routine, reassured them. 'Arrey, why are you worried? He has no doubt gone to perform the sandhya kala. Just wait a while. He will be back.'

As the people continued to talk among themselves, a cry rang out.

'Look, look! See, See! The bridegroom's father is coming back,' exclaimed a man who was standing at the edge of the crowd.

Everyone rushed to see what the man was pointing at. It was indeed Harjimal returning. He was strolling along leisurely and did not seem to be in a hurry. He smiled at the gathered crowd and waved in greeting.

The guests hurried towards him and surrounded him, all talking together at once. Harjimal was surprised at this reception. He looked from one to the other in bewilderment.

'Where did you go, Harjimal? We were all so worried. Thank God you are back,' said one man as he thumped him on the back.

'You left the *mandap* of your son's wedding and disappeared!' said another as he took Harjimal's arm to get his attention.

'Why did you not tell anyone where you were going? We were all worried about you,' said yet another man softly.

'We thought the wedding would not take place,' said one with a sly smile.

Harjimal was perplexed at the commotion. He held up his hands and requested the chattering guests to quieten down.

'Quiet, *bhai log*, quiet. As you can see, I am here. I had only gone to perform my sandhya kala. My family knows that I will not miss it, come what may. See, while you all are agitated, my family is calm. They know me,' said Harjimal with folded hands, thanking the guests for their concern. The people looked around and indeed, none of the family members seemed worried.

Harjimal then walked nonchalantly to the *mandap* and asked the pujari to resume the rites.

The pheras around the fire started and young Ramkrishna was married to Narbada.

His marriage to Narbada did not come in the way of Ramkrishna's quest for knowledge. A brilliant student with a laser-sharp mind, he excelled in mental mathematics, solving complex computations without the need for paper and pencil. While formal education in English was not available in Chirawa, Ramkrishna learnt the basics of the language through conversations and then taught other children around him.

As a preteen, Ramkrishna spent most of his time studying and looking after his family. His father was in Calcutta, and it was left to him, as the eldest male member of the family, to take care of them.

Ramkrishna had grown up with a somewhat entitled attitude. Until his brother, Jaidayal, was born, he was the only male child in a household of five women. They pampered him, and he was used to ordering them around. They, in turn, fulfilled his every wish. After his marriage, he directed his attention to his young bride, treating Narbada almost like a personal slave and expressing his sense of entitlement through her.

The family lived in rented accommodation, paying Rs 13 per month for a room with two verandas. A cot was placed in the bigger veranda for Ramkrishna's grandmother, while the room was shared by Ramkrishna's parents and siblings. The smaller veranda, just big enough to fit a cot, was used by Ramkrishna and Narbada for sleeping.

The smaller veranda faced north and did not receive any breeze. Due to their lack of finances, the family could not afford an electrical connection and thus had no electric fans. Ramkrishna would insist that Narbada fan him with a hand fan while he slept. The young girl did this dutifully without complaint, sometimes fanning her husband until as late as 2 a.m.

Ramkrishna also required Narbada to observe the *ghoonghat*. The young girl, again, obeyed her husband without a murmur,

Ramkrishna Gets Married and Runs Away from Home 23

keeping her head and face covered at all times. However, he went a step further, insisting that no part of her arm be visible, even while cooking, and would pinch it if it was exposed for even a moment. As a twelve-year-old preteen, Ramkrishna enjoyed the power he wielded over the young girl, who scurried to meet his every desire and order.

It was only in later years that he fully felt the burden of his misconduct towards his wife. He spent much of his life in remorse and never truly overcame the guilt of the ill-treatment he had inflicted upon her. In many of his writings, he confessed that he wished for forgiveness from Narbada.

Ramkrishna may have been a sharp boy, but he had a troubled mind. He believed in the scriptures and was deeply religious, yet he had a burning desire to get rich. Though he had been taught to treat all people with respect, he could not stop himself from treating his own wife almost like a personal servant. He knew he should spend more time learning and getting educated, but his mind constantly wandered in different directions. He wanted to enjoy all aspects of life, but at the same time, he believed in renunciation. An endless churn of conflicting emotions consumed him.

This turmoil plagued Ramkrishna. He was a tortured soul. He had no one to talk to about the dilemmas he faced. The more his inner conflict grew, the worse he behaved with Narbada.

When the disquiet in his mind became unbearable, Ramkrishna ran away from home. He wanted to spend some time alone to regain control over himself. One night, without informing anyone in the family, he left home.

He went to Sri Jagannath Puri, hoping that the deity would help him find the answers he was so desperately seeking. It was a long journey for the young boy to undertake on his own. The fact that Puri was close to Calcutta, where his father was, might have influenced Ramkrishna's choice of destination.

Back in Chirawa, the family was shocked when they discovered Ramkrishna was missing. No one had seen him go. No one had heard him go. They waited for a day, hoping he had gone somewhere in the neighbourhood. But after a couple of days passed with no sign of him, the family became worried.

Jadiya Devi asked Narbada if she had known that Ramkrishna was planning to go away. Poor Narbada could only cry and shake her head. The family thought that Ramkrishna would return in another day or two. They waited.

As more days passed without any trace of the young man, Jadiya Devi decided that it was time to inform her husband about Ramkrishna's disappearance. Harjimal was distraught, but he did not know where to even begin looking for his son.

As no one had any idea why Ramkrishna had left, they couldn't guess where he might have gone. His young wife was distraught and blamed herself for his running away. She, too, could not offer any suggestions about where to look for him.

Jadiya Devi took to her bed and refused all food. With great difficulty, Narbada forced her mother-in-law to at least drink water through the day. She would console Jadiya Devi by saying, 'Look at me. See how I am living without him, my husband. You must be strong.'

Ramkrishna, meanwhile, was living in Puri, sleeping in different *dharmashalas*—charitable rest houses. As Puri was a temple town, there was no dearth of *dharmashalas* for devotees. The temple provided *bhog*, or food, to anyone who wished to eat. Many devotees visiting the temple donated warm clothes and blankets, which were distributed to those in need. Ramkrishna, too, took a couple of blankets to keep himself warm.

By now, he had spent enough time on his own to mull over his inner turmoil and was beginning to find some peace. He began thinking about his family, especially his father. He wanted to return home but did not have the courage to do so. He knew that he had acted like a coward and was afraid that his family, particularly his father, would be angry with him and stop loving him.

Family was very important to Ramkrishna. He also wanted to make amends with Narbada. He knew he had treated her badly and wanted to atone for his behaviour. Yet, he did not know how to reunite with his family. He wished someone would magically find him in Puri.

One day, as he was taking a bath in the Chandan Talaab, an idea struck him as he looked at the gold chain around his neck. As soon as he completed his morning routine, he went to the post office. There, he took a packet and put his gold chain in it, and, for good measure, added his ring as well. He mailed the packet to his father in Calcutta. There was no note along with the jewellery. He justified this act to himself as an act of renunciation—by giving away the only valuables he had, he believed he was undergoing a process of penance. In reality, he hoped that his father would come to find him as the ornaments would prove that Ramkrishna was still alive.

Harjimal received the packet in the post. It seemed heavy. He weighed it in his hands as he wondered who had sent it and what was within. Upon opening it he instantly recognized the ornaments as belonging to his runaway son. For a moment, his heart sank as he assumed the worst. Then, rationality took over.

He examined the postmark closely and saw that the packet had been mailed from Puri. He asked an assistant to accompany him and immediately left for Puri, praying that he would find his son alive and well.

Ramkrishna was bathing in the Chandan Talaab when he heard someone shouting his name. His first thought was that it was someone from the rest house and that he may have forgotten his blanket there. But as he took a closer look at the two men approaching him, he recognized one of them—it was Harjimal.

Overcome with emotion, Ramkrishna burst into tears. It was as if all his pent-up emotions burst forth. He could not stop sobbing. He felt both fear and contrition. He was scared that his father would be angry—and at the same time he knew he had done something wrong by running away without informing anyone.

Harjimal and his assistant walked up to the sobbing Ramkrishna. Without saying a word, the older man enveloped his son in a tight hug. Ramkrishna clung to his father, still crying. Harjimal kept patting his son's back with one hand while ruffling his hair with the other. Gradually, Ramkrishna's sobs subsided and he began to take deep, gulping breaths. He tried to speak but could not.

Harjimal said nothing. He was waiting for his son to calm down.

'I am very sorry, Bapu. I am so sorry,' Ramkrishna said as soon as he was able to speak coherently. He continued to hold on to his father as if afraid that he would disappear if he let go.

'There, there, don't worry, son. All is well now,' Harjimal said as he continued to pat his son on the back.

Once the sobbing had stopped completely Harjimal took Ramkrishna by the hand and led him to a stone bench near the talaab. Father and son sat down, backs straight, gazing into the distance. Neither said a word.

Then Harjimal asked softly, 'What happened, son?'

This was enough for Ramkrishna to start speaking. He spoke rapidly as if a dam had burst within him. He told his father about his internal churn—the dilemmas he was facing, the contradictions between his thoughts and actions and his desire to find inner peace.

Harjimal let his son speak. He knew that Ramkrishna was undergoing a process. He also knew that his son was intelligent and would go far in life. The only obstacle to Ramkrishna reaching his full potential, ironically, was Ramkrishna himself. As the wiser and older man, Harjimal let Ramkrishna pour his heart out.

Once Ramkrishna finished speaking, he looked at peace. He felt a lightness within him, as if a great burden had been lifted from his shoulders. He looked at Harjimal with love and leaned across to hug his father.

'What is your plan now, son?' Harjimal asked, again softly, as he gently extricated himself from the embrace.

'You are not angry with me, Bapu?' asked Ramkrishna in a small voice. He was still afraid that his father would be angry with him.

'Not at all, son! What is there to be angry about? I am just happy that you are safe and sound,' Harjimal reassured him.

'Oh Bapu, I was so frightened,' Ramkrishna said in a rush.

'I hope you are not frightened now. So, tell me, what do you plan to do next?' Harjimal asked again, this time more firmly.

'I really don't know, Bapu. You tell me what to do,' said Ramkrishna as if he were a small boy once again.

'I would say, go back home to your wife and the rest of the family, son,' Said Harjimal.

At the mention of Narbada, Ramkrishna began crying again.

'Oh Bapu, I have been treating Narbada very badly. I am so ashamed of myself. How can I go back and face her? I want to stay here in Puri,' Ramkrishna said between small sobs.

Harjimal decided it was time to take charge. He shifted a little and distanced himself from his son on the bench. Half turning, he faced Ramkrishna.

'Son, it is time for you to go home,' he said firmly.

Ramkrishna opened his mouth to interrupt, but Harjimal silenced him with a gesture.

'Son, if you do not go back, you will regret it all your life. Your confusion was temporary. Maybe it was part of the growing up process. But now, you must go back.'

Ramkrishna listened intently as his father continued speaking.

'Son, a man has three duties in his life. The first is *yagya* to the *devtas*, the second is puja to the rishis and the third is *shraad* to the forefathers. Similarly, you have a duty towards your family, and if you do not fulfil it, your next life will be affected. So, it is better to return home and take charge of your responsibilities.'

Ramkrishna absorbed his father's advice.

'All right, Bapu. I will go home. I also promise to look after Narbada better. I will try to make her life more comfortable. I know I have been unfair to her.'

Harjimal patted him on the back, a gesture of encouragement and approval.

Ramkrishna Gets Married and Runs Away from Home

Ramkrishna went back home. However, he was not given the chance to atone for his bad behaviour towards his wife. Soon after his return, Narbada fell gravely ill. She suffered from bronchitis. When the local medics could not help her, she was sent to her father's house in Nawalgarh as the climate there was better. In spite of receiving good medical care at her parents' home, Narbada's health did not improve. She died at the young age of seventeen.

Ramkrishna was inconsolable and blamed himself for her death. He knew he had not been able to redeem himself in her eyes after his return from Puri. He could do nothing except bear the burden of guilt for the rest of his life.

After his wife's death, Ramkrishna moved to Calcutta to be with his father. By then, Harjimal had moved to Uttarpada, a suburb of Calcutta, where he had opened a cloth shop. Young Ramkrishna started working with his father. He would load his bicycle with bales of cloth and ride to Calcutta. There he would go door to door and lane by lane to sell cloth.

On his daily trips to Calcutta, Ramkrishna often found time to stop by the Hooghly River and watch the flowing water. Being near the river calmed him. He would also observe the fishermen returning with their nets full of fish. At first, Ramkrishna watched with horror and pity as the nets were emptied of their catch. Out of the water, the fish thrashed around wildly, seemingly gasping for breath and appearing to be in pain. Ramkrishna watched this scene daily with horrified fascination. In the beginning he would often cry at the plight of the fish, his heart filled with sorrow. However, as he watched the same scene being played out in front of him every day, he began to understand the concept of the survival of the fittest.

He understood the hierarchy of nature and the existence of a food chain.

This was one of his earliest lessons—that those at the bottom of the chain were vulnerable, while those at the top were strong. His resolve to climb up from the bottom of the chain to the top was further strengthened during those days by the banks of the river.

4

Ramkrishna Is Bitten by the Speculation Bug

RAMKRISHNA was only sixteen years old when Narbada passed away. The family wanted him to marry again, especially as there was no surviving child from the marriage. Although Ramkrishna was not keen on remarrying, he eventually agreed after much persuasion from the family, especially his mother. He remained in Calcutta with his father while the family looked for a suitable bride.

Harjimal, meanwhile, had closed his cloth shop and returned to salaried employment. He got a job with Brij Raj Harsukh Rai, earning Rs 60 a month. Ramkrishna also found a job. It was with his maternal uncle, Seth Motilal, who was a bullion trader. He earned Rs 50 a month, which was enough for a single young man to make a modest living.

However, Ramkrishna did not remain single for long. The search for a suitable girl continued in Chirawa. One proposal was for a girl from a good family, who was slim and presentable and approved by Ramkrishna's mother. However, Ramkrishna refused the match when he found out that the girl's brother was lame. Another proposal came from a wealthy girl of the Patodia family. This time it was Harjimal who refused as he suspected the girl had a defect in one of her eyes.

Finally, a betrothal was arranged with Durga, a simple girl who could read and write. Ramkrishna found her less intelligent than Narbada but liked her willingness to learn. The two were married in 1910, and Durga went on to remain by Ramkrishna's side as his wife for more than forty-five years.

Harjimal was keen to see a grandchild, but it was not to be. He died in 1913, three years after Ramkrishna and Durga were married. The young couple had been unable to have a surviving child as Durga's health remained delicate.

After Harjimal passed away, Ramkrishna became the man of the house. He was only twenty years old at the time. He was working in Calcutta and saw little sense in maintaining two separate households. He moved his household—which included his grandmother, mother, brother and Durga—to Calcutta.

As a single man, his salary of Rs 50 per month had been enough to meet his needs; but with a family of five adults, the money was barely enough. The room his father had rented was too small, so Ramkrishna began looking for larger accommodation. He could not afford to rent an entire house on his meagre salary. He eventually found a room that was just large enough to fit five people and little else. Even so, the rent consumed almost a quarter of his monthly salary. His brother, eleven years younger, was still a boy and unable to contribute to the family income. As for the women in the family, there was no question of them working to earn money.

Ramkrishna may not have had a formal higher education, but life had taught him to be street smart. He had a sharp mind with a head for numbers. Another advantage, as he discovered, was his rudimentary knowledge of the English language. Living in Calcutta, he learnt more English and also picked up Bengali. At first, he learnt the new language by reading the billboards and shop signs he saw every day. As he interacted with the locals, he started speaking the language as well.

Ramkrishna's maternal uncle, Seth Motilal, the bullion trader, dealt in ounces, trading in small lots. He received silver rates daily from Bombay and used them to sell the metal in the local market at a markup. Motilal had rented a small room near the telegraph office, which enabled him to receive the telegraphed silver rates quickly. Traders with access to the rates before others could earn more profit. Much like the price of shares and stocks, prior knowledge of the price allowed a trader to decide whether to sell or purchase and make money.

For instance, if Motilal knew that the rate in Bombay was lower than the prevailing rate in Calcutta, he would sell part of his stock at the higher local rate. Once the market became aware of the Bombay rate, the price of silver would fall. At that time, Motilal would buy back some of the stock at the lower rate. The spread between the selling and buying price was the profit he made.

Since the First World War had begun, metal prices on the exchange had been fluctuating, sometimes wildly. Therefore, knowledge of price movements was essential to decide whether to buy or sell in the market. Prices were set by the London

Metal Exchange, and traders around the world, including in India, used that as the benchmark for their own local prices.

Ramkrishna's job at his uncle's office was to take the rates received via telegraph by Bhuwanlal, one of Motilal's staff, and deliver them to his uncle. Bhuwanlal was stationed at the telegraph office, waiting for the messages to come in. The telegraphs were in English, which Bhuwanlal could not read—but Ramkrishna could. Unbeknownst to anyone, Ramkrishna would open the envelope and read the messages on his way to his uncle. He soon developed an understanding of the silver market. He also began analysing daily events and predicting the price of silver in the coming days. He observed that certain events or news created optimism in the market, leading to higher prices; similarly, certain developments led to bearish sentiments in the market.

Ramkrishna started playing a game with himself. Each day, before he read the telegraph, he would predict whether the price had risen, fallen or remained flat. He enjoyed the game as it challenged him mentally. On days when he correctly predicted the price trend, he went over his decision-making process to understand what he had got right. On days when he got it wrong, he reviewed his thought process to figure out which events or news items he had failed to analyse properly. With his sharp mind, he steadily improved his ability to assess domestic and international events and accordingly predict silver prices, to the point where it became almost intuitive. Of course, no one can perfectly predict market movements, and there was always a margin of error, but Ramkrishna became more confident over time.

Since his childhood, Ramkrishna had been restless—restless to achieve more, to earn more money and to restore

Ramkrishna Is Bitten by the Speculation Bug

the respect his great-grandfather had commanded. He did not like working for his uncle, but he also knew that he had to. He did not complain to anyone, especially to his family, about his situation, but he indeed wanted to lift them out of poverty. Inside him was a keen, ambitious mind, restrained by his family's circumstances. He was astute enough to understand that survival came before anything else. Yet, his mind constantly churned, seeking opportunities that might present themselves.

One such opportunity arose when Ramkrishna read a telegram from Bombay and realized that the price of silver had increased significantly. Instead of going straight to his uncle's office, he went to Dalamal Saraf, another silver dealer in the local market.

'Ram-Ram Sethji,' said Ramkrishna as he walked into Dalamal's shop.

Dalamal had just opened his shop for the day and was alone—none of his attendants or staff had arrived yet. Ramkrishna knew this and had therefore chosen this time to meet Dalamal. He did not want others around.

Dalamal was organizing his desk in preparation for the day. When Ramkrishna walked in, Dalamal had his back to the door. He was beating the dust out of a cushion, swearing softly at his absent staff for doing a poor job of cleaning.

Hearing Ramkrishna's voice, Dalamal turned. When he saw who it was, he put down the cushion, his anger forgotten. He liked Ramkrishna. In fact, most people in the market liked him. The young man had a pleasing personality, even though he was nothing great to look at. He treated everyone with respect and always had an interesting tale to share.

'Arrey Ramkrishna, *kaise ho*? Is all well? What are you doing here so early in the morning?' asked Dalamal, smiling widely. He cleared a space on a low chair by sweeping aside some clutter and gestured for Ramkrishna to sit.

As Ramkrishna took his seat, Dalamal, too, sat down on his cushion, the accumulated dust notwithstanding. He looked around to ask someone to get water for his guest, but realized there was no one else in the shop.

'I'm sorry Ramkrishna, I can't offer you water just now. As you can see, the staff hasn't arrived yet,' said Dalamal, spreading his hands wide to indicate the empty shop.

'Don't worry, Sethji, I have not come for water,' said Ramkrishna as he sat and looked around the shop with interest.

'Never mind, never mind. Tell me what I can do for you,' asked Dalamal expansively, assuming that Ramkrishna needed something.

'Sethji, I don't need anything from you. But I might have something that could be of interest to you,' said Ramkrishna, patting the pocket where the envelope from the telegraph office was tucked.

Dalamal's interest was piqued. He leaned forward. 'What is it, my boy? What do you have that might be of interest to me?' he asked, glancing at the pocket.

'Sethji, I can give you the silver prices from Bombay. You can use the information to make a lot of money,' said Ramkrishna, an impish gleam in his eyes.

'You have the price? What is it? Tell me, Ramkrishna. Is it up or down?' The trader in Dalamal was interested at once.

'I'll tell you, Sethji, but you have to promise not to tell my uncle that I shared this with you. He will get angry,' said

Ramkrishna Is Bitten by the Speculation Bug

Ramkrishna, still patting his pocket but not taking out the envelope yet.

'Then why are you telling me about the price? Do you want something in return?' asked Dalamal, leaning back as if losing interest.

'No, no, Sethji. I want nothing. You have always been kind to me, and I wanted to repay that kindness,' said Ramkrishna quickly, the sincere look on his face reassuring Dalamal.

'All right, all right, now I'm really keen to know what the price of silver is. Tell me quickly,' urged Dalamal, reaching out to grip Ramkrishna's arm.

Ramkrishna revealed the price as written in the telegraph. Dalamal's eyes widened as he realized that he could make a substantial amount of money thanks to this information. However, he had a doubt.

'Who else have you told about this? Does your uncle know?' Dalamal asked with a speculative look in his eyes.

'No one else knows, Sethji. Uncle will find out in the next fifteen minutes, but I haven't told anyone else,' Ramkrishna assured the older man.

Dalamal was delighted with the price-sensitive information. He jumped up from his seat and rushed towards Ramkrishna. The young man stood up in confusion, unsure why the older man was coming towards him. He took two steps back.

Dalamal reached Ramkrishna and hugged him tightly before lifting the skinny young man off the ground in his embrace.

'Many, many thanks, Ramkrishna, for this information. I must quickly get to work and use it,' Dalamal was clearly eager to get to work.

'All right, Sethji. I hope the day goes well with you,' said Ramkrishna, turning to leave the shop.

'One moment, Ramkrishna, one moment. Just wait a minute,' said Dalamal as he quickly opened a drawer in his desk. He rummaged around and pulled out a handful of currency notes. He held them out to Ramkrishna, who looked at Dalamal quizzically.

'Take this, Ramkrishna. This is not a bribe, but a token of my gratitude for giving me this valuable information,' said Dalamal.

'Sethji, I cannot take this. It wouldn't be right,' protested Ramkrishna meekly, without much conviction.

But Dalamal would hear none of it. He forced Ramkrishna to accept the currency notes.

As Ramkrishna stuffed the money into his pocket, he looked at Dalamal, who was now clearly eager for him to leave.

'Sethji, please do not tell anyone that you got this information from me,' said Ramkrishna as he folded his hands and turned to leave.

'Of course, of course, no one will know. Now run along, I have a lot of work to do,' replied Dalamal brusquely, already focused on the day's work ahead.

'And come and see me again soon, Ramkrishna,' Dalamal called out as Ramkrishna walked out of the shop.

Ramkrishna had hoped for a result like this. He had anticipated being compensated for bringing price-sensitive information to the trader, and the money in his pocket made him happy.

The experience made Ramkrishna realize that he could earn a bit on the side by passing on price information to other traders. He knew, however, that he had to keep this group small because what he was doing was, technically, wrong. As an employee of his uncle, any information related to his work had to be passed on to Motilal alone.

Still, greed got the better of him. Ramkrishna rationalized his actions by convincing himself that technically, his uncle was not suffering any losses from this arrangement.

Motilal was still able to trade based on the information and was not, in any way, negatively impacted by his nephew sharing the same details with a handful of people. Thus, Ramkrishna continued to pass on the information to a select group of traders, earning a commission for his efforts. He swore all of them to secrecy, imploring them not to let his uncle know that it was he who had given them the price information.

But this arrangement was not to last long. The trader community in Calcutta was a small one, and the Marwaris all knew one other. Motilal had been puzzled by the activity in the silver market. He had realized that there were other traders who seemed to have the same information as he did before the market officially opened. He asked Bhuwanlal if any other trader had stationed their staff at the telegraph office, but Bhuwanlal confirmed there was no one else. He started asking around the market, and to his shock, discovered that Ramkrishna had been sharing the price information with other traders before coming in to the office.

At first, Motilal could not believe it. But as more people told him the same thing, he became furious.

'Ramkrishna, who do you think you are?'

Motilal was sitting in his office when he saw his nephew walk into the office. Without even getting up he shouted angrily at Ramkrishna. Continuing to glare at him threateningly, Motilal rose from his seat and walked towards the younger man.

Ramkrishna immediately realized what had happened. He knew the game was up. Prepared to apologize to his uncle, he opened his mouth to speak, but Motilal didn't give him a chance.

He stood before Ramkrishna, fuming with anger. Seeing that Ramkrishna was trying to speak, he gestured sharply with a thrust of his hand to silence him.

'Ramkrishna, who do you think you are, eh? You think you are the lord and master of someplace? Let me tell you exactly who you are. You are a nobody. You hear me? You are a nobody. You have no father, no money, and yet you have illusions of grandeur? Who do you think you are? *Tumhari aukaat kya hai?*' Motilal shouted, his voice shaking with anger.

His staff cowered and stayed away, though they listened intently. Ramkrishna stood there—not with eyes downcast but with a trace of defiance in them. He had been prepared to accept his mistake and seek his uncle's forgiveness. But the manner in which his uncle was shouting and the harshness of his words hurt Ramkrishna's pride and self-esteem.

'Uncle, let me say ... ' Ramkrishna began as Motilal paused to take a breath. But his uncle was not finished. Motilal cut him off.

'You know, if it were not for me, you would be on the streets, Ramkrishna. It is I who took pity on you and gave you a job here. It is my money that is allowing you to maintain your family. If I throw you out, you will all die penniless,' Motilal continued, his anger unabated.

'Uncle, you may be angry with me, but just listen to me. Let me explain ... ' Ramkrishna tried to get in a few words.

Motilal was on a roll, his eyes blazing and arms akimbo. He was in no mood to listen to Ramkrishna.

'No, you listen to me, young man. You listen to me,' he said, wagging his finger in Ramkrishna's face. 'It is only because of my sister that I am not physically throwing you out. But for you, I have nothing but contempt. Living on my charity and then stabbing me in the back! Who does that? Who?' Motilal demanded, looking around at the rest of the staff, as if seeking validation for his anger.

Ramkrishna was now angry. From contrition he moved to seething rage. He was upset by Motilal's references to his poverty.

He straightened his back and drew himself up to his full height. Even though he was several inches shorter than Motilal, he stared back defiantly at the older man. Motilal saw something in his nephew's eyes and quietened down.

'Uncle, I may have been in the wrong, but you had no right to say what you did. I may be poor, but I have my self-respect. Let me also say this with all humility—I am perfectly capable of looking after my family. I do not need handouts or charity from you. I am leaving. And one day, you will see what my "aukaat" is,' Ramkrishna said calmly but firmly.

With his head held high and his back straight, Ramkrishna walked out of his uncle's office. Motilal's staff watched him go with admiration in their eyes. They, too, were poor and Ramkrishna's declaration of self-respect despite his poverty resonated with them. Ramkrishna had never treated them badly, and in spite of his limited means, had helped them whenever they were in need. They wished him well.

5

Lady Luck Finally Smiles on Ramkrishna

RAMKRISHNA was concerned about his future but not overly worried. He had saved a little money thanks to his side activities. He spoke with his mother about the situation.

'Why are you worried, Ramkrishna? We are used to living with less money. If you return to your job, we can live easily on fifty rupees a month,' Jadiya Devi said, quick to reassure her son.

'But Mother, I do not want to work with Uncle. He insulted me—just like my grandfather was insulted. Please don't ask me to go back there. I will find a way to make it work,' Ramkrishna said plaintively.

'I understand son, I understand. I know how important respect is to you. I only suggested it because you seemed upset about losing the job,' Jadiya Devi replied gently.

'Not at all, Mother. Trust me, I will find a way out of this difficulty,' said Ramkrishna confidently.

Jadiya Devi smiled and affectionately patted her son on the head.

Ramkrishna had been going to the telegraph office for years to collect messages containing the silver prices in Bombay, and during that time, he had made friends there. Making friends came easily to him. Since childhood, people had responded positively to his sunny disposition. Word about Motilal sacking Ramkrishna had quickly spread through the market. When people met him, they began offering advice on what he could do next. One common theme emerged from these conversations: Ramkrishna lacked the capital to build assets for a business. He needed to look for options that were asset light. He knew his greatest asset was his sharp mind and strong understanding of numbers. He decided that speculation, or playing the *satta* market, was his best option.

Ramkrishna started speculating in the Calcutta market, beginning with small amounts as his funds were limited. He soon found that he was good at it. He had a speculator's mind, and he enjoyed the process. Whether it was beginner's luck or his sharp intellect, he made initial gains. And then greed took over.

Ramkrishna started betting larger amounts in the satta bazaar. A person with significant responsibilities might have been cautious with their earnings from the market, but Ramkrishna was a gambler at heart. With the First World War raging, the commodities market was fluctuating wildly. Even seasoned speculators found it difficult to consistently bet right, and Ramkrishna was a speculator who had yet to earn the label of 'seasoned'.

He lost money in the market, but instead of cutting his losses, he put in more money. The habit of speculation is addictive, and Ramkrishna found himself caught in its grip. He borrowed money from friends and relatives to feed his addiction. Sometimes he won and at other times he lost.

It is well-known that speculators in the market go through cycles of fasting and feasting—periods of losses followed by periods of gains. Unfortunately, Ramkrishna had been in a fasting phase for some time. Yet, like every gambler, he believed that the feasting days were just around the corner. Thus, he continued playing the satta bazaar.

Meanwhile, there was finally some good news at home. His wife, Durga, was pregnant and had not suffered a miscarriage. Despite being married for over six years, Durga had been unable to carry a pregnancy to full term. This had weakened her health, and the family had been concerned. Now, with this new pregnancy progressing well, the family was determined to do all they could to help Durga.

Their care bore fruit when Durga gave birth to a daughter in 1917. The first child in the family was named Rama.

This was also the time when Ramkrishna was going through a particularly bad phase in the market. He was losing money and had been unable to repay the loans he had taken from friends and family. Indebted and with no money in hand, he was labelled a defaulter by the market. No one wanted to deal with him, and no one was ready to loan him even five rupees. This rankled and weighed heavily on Ramkrishna's mind.

One incident, in particular, troubled him deeply. He had suffered yet another round of losses and owed a broker Rs 500. The broker kept asking for his money back, but Ramkrishna was unable to repay him.

One day, as he was walking through the market, Ramkrishna saw the broker approaching him. Knowing that the man would ask for the money he didn't have, Ramkrishna prepared to explain the situation to the broker. However, he was taken aback by the other man's actions.

The broker pulled the long scarf from around his neck and threw it around Ramkrishna's. Stunned into silence, Ramkrishna stood immobile as the broker tightened the scarf around his neck like a leash.

By now, people had started gathering around the two men. Both were familiar faces in the market and the scene generated a lot of interest.

Ramkrishna was humiliated. If there was one thing that was important to him, it was his respect—especially in the eyes of others. Yet here he was, tied up like an animal by the broker. He knew this was all because of the money he owed. At that moment, more than ever, he wished desperately that he had money.

The broker was enjoying his moment in the spotlight. He kept playing with the scarf leash, pulling and pushing it in different directions. Ramkrishna, determined not to fall and further humiliate himself in the eyes of the ever-growing crowd, kept moving to maintain his balance.

'Let me go, bhai, let me go. I promise I will pay back your money,' Ramkrishna pleaded.

The broker laughed loudly. He pulled at the leash, causing Ramkrishna to stumble, and looked around at the crowd triumphantly.

'Look at this man. He says he will pay me back. But does he even know where will he get the money from? I made a mistake loaning him the money, but this time, he's not getting away,' he declared as he continued to pull at the leash causing Ramkrishna to keep stumbling.

Ramkrishna was well-liked in the market. Though he was poor in terms of money, he was rich in personality and had many friends. A couple of the gathered men tried to intervene.

'Arrey bhai, let the poor man go. Why are you humiliating him like this?' said one man.

'Do you think this *naatak* will get you your money? Let him go, and I'm sure he will return your money,' added another.

The broker turned on the second man with a sneer. 'If you're so sure that he will return the money, why don't you give me the money and then wait for him to give it back to you? Eh? Will you do that?'

As the second man fell silent, the broker became more aggressive. 'Tell me, when will you return my money, you miserable man?' he demanded loudly.

Ramkrishna had closed his eyes and was praying silently. At the broker's question, he opened his eyes and looked straight at him. 'Bhai sahib, I've told you that I will return your money very soon. Trust me. Ask anyone here—have I ever kept anyone's money? I have not. I will repay you too. Please release me. This is not right.'

The broker remained unmoved. Ramkrishna folded his hands and appealed again.

'If you keep me leashed like this, how will I find the money? Let me go, and trust me—I may be poor and without money now, but I am a man of my word. You will get your money back, I promise you. Please, just let me go.' Ramkrishna wanted the ordeal to end.

By now, a few elder traders in the market had arrived to watch the commotion. Two or three of them walked up to the broker and had a quiet word with him. Whatever they said seemed to have an effect; the broker looked sheepish. He nodded to the older men and let go of the scarf.

Ramkrishna immediately removed the scarf from around his neck and threw it to the ground. He nodded in gratitude to the older men and walked away. Though he felt like crying—in anger and frustration—he held back his tears. He refused to show any weakness before the whole market.

This public humiliation hurt Ramkrishna deeply. He was a proud man, and his heritage meant everything to him. To a Marwari, one's name is more valuable than money, and being humiliated in front of the community made Ramkrishna even more resolute to win back all he had lost. He just did not know how.

Fate decided to take matters into her own hands.

One day, after kissing his newborn daughter on the forehead, Ramkrishna went to the market. He did not know what he was going to do or whom he would try to meet. All he knew was that he wanted his luck to turn. He feet led him to an astrologer. Pandit Motiram Biala of Fatehpur was well-known in the area for his accurate predictions based on his reading of the stars.

On the way, Ramkrishna ran into an acquaintance. 'Where are you off to in such a rush, Ramkrishna?' the man asked.

'I am going to see Panditji,' replied Ramkrishna, shifting his cloth bag from one shoulder to the other.

'Oh, you mean Motiramji?' said the acquaintance, clearly in the mood for some chit-chat.

'Yes,' Ramkrishna answered curtly, eager to move on.

'Well, you know what they say—hunger drives people to the astrologer and the overfed run to the physician!' the man said, bursting into a cackle of laughter, his paan-stained teeth shining red in the morning sun.

'Okay, okay, you've had your fun. I am in a hurry,' replied Ramkrishna briskly, without a smile, as he walked away from the still-cackling man.

Pandit Motiram was a man of pious and saintly disposition. Ramkrishna also considered him a friend.

'What brings you here this morning, Ramkrishna?' asked Motiram with a big smile. He was very fond of the young man.

'Panditji, nothing seems to be going right for me. I need some astral help,' Ramkrishna said, wringing his hands in anguish.

Motiram realized that the young man was troubled. He walked up to him and gently patted him on the shoulder.

'Arrey bhai, Lakshmi has just come to your house. What are you so worried about?' said Motiram with a smile, hoping to dispel Ramkrishna's despondency.

'What do you mean, Panditji?' asked Ramkrishna, perplexed. He stopped wringing his hands and looked at Motiram with furrowed brows.

'Rama—your daughter Rama. She is Lakshmi, isn't she? She has brought good fortune to your family,' said Motiram. As an astrologer, he had a sense for these things.

Ramkrishna was stunned into silence.

'What do you mean? Rama? She has brought good fortune? Are you sure?' he asked, a rush of questions spilling out as soon as he found his voice.

'Haan bhai haan. I am sure,' said Pandit Motiram. 'But show me your horoscope, and I'll confirm it,' he added.

Ramkrishna had carried his horoscope with him and, taking it out carefully from his bag, handed it to Pandit Motiram. Fishing out his spectacles from his kurta pocket, Pandit

Lady Luck Finally Smiles on Ramkrishna

Motiram began studying the horoscope. Ramkrishna sat quietly, watching the bent head of his friend.

Pandit Motiram pored over the papers. As he moved his finger from one place to the other on the paper, he nodded as if in confirmation. His lips curled into a slow smile, and he looked up at Ramkrishna with a gleam in his eye before going back to studying the horoscope.

Ramkrishna grew impatient.

'What are you studying so seriously, Panditji?' he asked, standing above the seated man. He fidgeted with his hands as if urging Motiram to hurry.

'I am seeing your good fortune,' Motiram looked up and smiled at Ramkrishna.

'Now, don't make fun of a poor man, Panditji. I am in trouble, and you are mocking me,' Ramkrishna grumbled.

Pandit Motiram finally stopped examining the horoscope. He folded the papers and put his spectacles back in his pocket. As he handed the papers back to Ramkrishna, he smiled.

'My dear friend, your bad time is behind you. Good fortune is around the corner,' he said, patting his young friend on the arm.

'Can you explain more, please,' Ramkrishna asked. He desperately wanted to believe the astrologer but was still hesitant.

'Ramkrishna, you will get one lakh rupees in the sub-period of Budh (Mercury), in about a month and a half,' declared Pandit Motiram confidently.

Ramkrishna was dumbfounded, unable to say a word. One lakh rupees was a huge sum at the time (in the 1910s, it was equivalent to several tens of crores or more in modern terms).

'I have no credit in the market, and people have no faith in me. How on earth do you think this can even come true?' he asked incredulously when he finally found his voice, clutching the cloth bag tightly as if protecting the horoscope predicting his good fortune. He wanted desperately to believe his friend but could not.

Pandit Motiram assured him that the reading of the charts predicted that Ramkrishna would come into great wealth soon.

'If you don't believe me, I am willing to write it down for you, Ramkrishna,' offered Pandit Motiram.

Ramkrishna nodded wordlessly.

Motiram went to his writing station and pulled out a sheet of paper. He wrote a note prophesying that Ramkrishna would receive one lakh rupees soon. He signed the note with a flourish and handed it to Ramkrishna.

Ramkrishna was astounded. He knew that he had no hope of getting even one hundred rupees in the market, let alone a vast sum like one lakh. Still, he had the piece of paper with the prophesy written on it. He tucked it into his pocket and returned to his world of miseries.

Although Ramkrishna did not claim to have unwavering faith in God, he had developed faith in chanting Ram-Naam since childhood. Ram-Naam held special meaning for him, especially during trying times. It had become a habit for Ramkrishna to chant the name of Ram mentally, even while eating, drinking or going about his daily tasks. It was in this chanting of Ram Naam that Ramkrishna took solace after his meeting with Pandit Motiram.

Days passed and nothing out of the ordinary happened. Then, one day, out of the blue, Ramkrishna received a cable from one of his agents in London. The cable informed him that

Lady Luck Finally Smiles on Ramkrishna

silver prices were about to witness an abnormal increase on the London Metal Exchange. It was wartime, and the prices of metals were fluctuating wildly. Ramkrishna had dealt with this agent in the past and trusted his information.

Armed with the cable and its vital information, Ramkrishna went to the market to seek funds for speculating in silver. However, such was his credibility that no one was willing to even speak to him. He entreated several merchants to at least use the information for their own benefit, but all he received were mocking laughs and sneers.

Dejected and tired after being rejected by every merchant and trader in the Calcutta market, Ramkrishna trudged back home for dinner. Once home, he went to see Rama, his daughter. As he took her in his arms, a feeling of peace washed over him. Cradling her, Ramkrishna remembered his friend Pandit Motiram's words about Rama being like Lakshmi who had come to their house.

He decided to go back to Pandit Motiram, and handing Rama over to Durga, rushed off to see the astrologer.

'Panditji, look here, see what I have!' said Ramkrishna excitedly, waving the cable in front of his friend's face.

'Slow down, slow down, Ramkrishna. Tell me, what is it?' Motiram asked, surprised by Ramkrishna's late-night visit.

Ramkrishna showed Pandit Motiram the cable.

'What is this, Ramkrishna? I don't understand it at all,' said Motiram as he looked at the numbers on the telegraph. While the numbers on a horoscope made perfect sense to him, these figures seemed like gibberish.

'I will explain, Panditji,' Ramkrishna assured him as he pulled out a chair and gestured for Motiram to sit.

He then began explaining the basics of speculation.

He told Motiram that if the price of silver were to go up, as the cable suggested, one could make money by buying silver now and selling it later at the higher price. However, the full amount of money for the purchase was not required upfront. Only a small amount, known as margin money, was needed. Once the price of silver went up, it could be sold on the exchange. The difference between the purchase price and the sale price would be the profit.

Ramkrishna further explained that if he did the trade on his own and there was a loss, he would lose about Rs 50—the amount he usually earned as commission when he did business with traders. He admitted that he could not afford such a loss since it was the only money he had to support his family.

'So, what do you want from me, Ramkrishna?' asked Motiram.

'Panditji, I am asking you to do the trade. You have the money, and I can act as your agent. My commission will be Rs 100. The profit will be all yours,' said Ramkrishna. He had complete faith in the London agent's information and was certain there was a lot of money to be made if the price of silver went up.

'Yes, I have the money, but I've never done this before,' the astrologer hesitated a little.

'Don't worry, Panditji. Just follow my advice,' Ramkrishna urged, encouraging the older man.

The astrologer finally agreed to make a purchase on the Exchange for a sum of GBP 7,500. At the time, the Indian rupee was equivalent to the British pound. Thus, Motiram had committed Rs 7,500.

Ramkrishna was delighted. He had a deal and considered the commission he would earn to be a large sum of money.

Lady Luck Finally Smiles on Ramkrishna

Suddenly, he smacked his forehead and bit his tongue.

'What is it, Ramkrishna? Is something wrong?' asked Motiram quickly on seeing Ramkrishna's gestures.

'No, no, Panditji, everything is fine. It's just that I must send a cable to London to confirm the deal, but I just realized that I don't have the ten rupees needed to dispatch it,' Ramkrishna admitted.

The astrologer smiled indulgently and gave Ramkrishna ten rupees to send the cable.

Ramkrishna boarded a tram and hurried to the post office. He dispatched the cable to London and then returned home.

The next morning, as was his routine, Ramkrishna went to the river for his early morning dip. On his way, he saw a man who worked with Motiram coming towards him. The man gestured that he wanted to speak with Ramkrishna.

'Ram-Ram, bhai,' Ramkrishna called out in greeting, assuming Motiram had sent him for an update on the silver trade.

'Ramkrishna bhai, Panditji has sent word that he has changed his mind about the deal. He wants out,' said the worker.

'No, no, you're mistaken, bhai. Panditji himself told me to go ahead yesterday. You must be confused. Why don't you go back and check with him?' Ramkrishna replied confidently.

'No, Ramkrishna, it is you who are mistaken,' the man retorted irritably. He had been instructed by Motiram to tell Ramkrishna that he had changed his mind, and here was Ramkrishna insisting otherwise.

'Oh my God, this can't be true. Why would he do this to me?' Ramkrishna exclaimed, staring at the worker.

The worker merely shrugged, as if to say, *How would I know?* and walked away.

Ramkrishna was in a state of panic. He understood how the trade worked—he had put in the order, and now he was responsible for the transaction. But he had no money to cover it.

Forgetting about his morning dip, Ramkrishna gathered up his dhoti and ran to the astrologer's house.

Motiram, seeing Ramkrishna rushing towards his house, tried to beat a hasty retreat. He did not want to confront him. But Ramkrishna gave him no chance.

'Panditji, Panditji, what is this I hear? You're cancelling the deal? Surely this can't be true!' Ramkrishna spoke between gulps of air. He had run towards Motilal's house and was out of breath. He bent over slightly, holding his stomach, trying to catch his breath.

Motiram stood quietly, waiting for Ramkrishna to calm down. He then gestured for the young man to sit. Although Ramkrishna had quietened externally, his mind was churning. He asked again if Motiram had changed his mind.

Motiram looked at him calmly and confirmed that he did not want to go ahead with the silver deal.

'But why, Panditji, why? It's such a good deal. What made you change your mind?' Ramkrishna cried out in anguish. He was close to tears.

Motiram started to say something but then stopped. Seeing Ramkrishna's expectant look, he decided to continue.

'Ramkrishna, I will tell you, but you won't like it,' Motiram said softly. He was still fond of the young man.

'I am already feeling so bad, Panditji, that I don't think anything you say can make me feel worse. So, go ahead and tell me,' Ramkrishna replied petulantly.

'You know, Ramkrishna, I was genuinely excited about the silver deal. After you left, some friends came over to meet me. I guess my excitement was apparent, and they asked me what the reason was. So, I told them,' explained Motiram as he paced the room.

'Oh, but why did you tell your friends? Now they will also want to do similar deals. I was the only one with that information in all of Calcutta. And now you've shared it with others,' Ramkrishna exclaimed, still thinking only of the silver deal.

'No, no, Ramkrishna, no one else wants to do the deal. In fact, not only do they not want to do it, but they have also advised me against it,' said Motiram as he stopped pacing, turned and looked at the young man sitting on the chair.

Ramkrishna was utterly confused. He believed he had access to a good deal, and now he was being told that no one wanted to do it. He looked at Motiram, his eyes full of questions. The astrologer was visibly uncomfortable. He did not want to say more but knew he had to finish what he had started.

'The thing is, Ramkrishna, your reputation in the market is almost zero. My friends, all of them, were aghast at the fact that I had trusted you. They called you a no-good-doer. They even said that if I gave you the money, you wouldn't use it for the deal but to pay off your existing debts,' Motiram said, looking everywhere except at Ramkrishna.

Ramkrishna was stunned. What hurt him more wasn't what Motiram's friends had said but that Motiram—a man he considered a friend—had believed that the deal was a fraud.

'So, you too think that I would take your money and run away with it? That I would cheat you?' asked Ramkrishna in a small voice.

'No, no, no, Ramkrishna!' Motiram was quick to defend himself.

'Then why, Panditji? Why?' asked Ramkrishna again in anguish.

'Ramkrishna, you must believe me—I told my friends you are not the type of person who would take my money and cheat me. But they said even if I went through with the deal and made a profit, you wouldn't share all of it with me. On the other hand, if there were a loss, I would have to bear the entire burden,' explained Motiram.

'You know I would never do anything like that, Panditji,' Ramkrishna assured him desperately.

Motiram nodded.

'I know, Ramkrishna, I know. But what to do? My friends have made up my mind for me. I'm sorry, but I will not go ahead with the silver trade,' said Motiram firmly.

No amount of explanations, promises or entreaties from Ramkrishna could persuade the astrologer to change his mind. Realizing it was futile to stay any longer, Ramkrishna left Motiram's house after assuring him that he, the astrologer, would not be held responsible for the transaction.

As he walked away, dejected, Ramkrishna let out a wry laugh. He found it ironic that the astrologer who had predicted such a bright future for him was unable to believe in it himself!

Ramkrishna was a broken man when he left Motiram's house. In despair, he went straight to the river, hoping to find solace in the water. He was in the habit of performing the Gayatri Japa—chanting the Gayatri Mantra—while standing in the river. That morning, Ramkrishna performed the ritual with greater earnestness and for twice the usual duration.

Yet, it seemed as though the gods had failed to listen to his earnest prayers.

When Ramkrishna returned home, he found a cable waiting for him. It informed him that the transaction for GBP 7,500 the previous day had been completed. However, contrary to expectations, the silver market had fallen, and Ramkrishna had incurred a loss of GBP 3,000.

Ramkrishna was in no position to rustle up such a large sum of money. He sent a message to say that he could not square up the deal and resigned himself to waiting to see what Destiny had in store for him. The prediction made by his friend now seemed even more distant than ever.

There was nothing Ramkrishna could do but wait. He had no idea whether his losses would increase or decrease. All he knew was that he did not have the money needed to settle the deal.

Destiny, however, seemed to have decided that it was time for the astrologer's prediction to come true!

Two days later, Ramkrishna received information that the market trend had reversed, and the price of silver had risen significantly. The agent from the London Metal Exchange sent a cable asking if Ramkrishna wanted to settle the trade.

Ramkrishna reviewed the numbers. If he settled, he stood to make a neat profit of GBP 4,000 after repaying Motiram the original GBP 7,500. In his mind, keeping the entire profit for himself was justified, as the astrologer had cancelled the deal the very next day.

At this stage, it would have been prudent for Ramkrishna to square up the deal. However, he was a speculator at heart. The thrill of speculation excited and energized him. He forgot the days of his misery and was eager to speculate on the rising market. But he had no money. He could have secured his share of the profit by settling the deal, but he chose not to.

With no money in hand and yet wanting to speculate in hopes of earning more, Ramkrishna went home and stole the only piece of jewellery his wife, Durga, had left. He knew that if he had asked her, Durga would not have objected. However, Ramkrishna did not have the courage to ask. He knew that what he was doing was wrong, but he could not help himself.

Armed with the money from selling the jewellery, Ramkrishna sent a cable to another agent in London, instructing him to purchase silver worth GBP 10,000. The market rose again, and Ramkrishna's profits increased to GBP 20,000. Although this was only paper profit, Ramkrishna used it to buy even more silver through a third agent.

The market continued to rise, and Ramkrishna's profits kept increasing. In his saner moments, he realized the situation was akin to continuously inflating a rubber balloon—if it was overinflated, it would inevitably burst. Ramkrishna understood that the bursting of the silver bubble would be a disaster.

He had no friends he could confide in, and the astrologer, whom he had once considered a friend, was no longer an option. Feeling the pressure of his actions, Ramkrishna finally confessed to his mother and wife. However, even then, he was economical with the truth. He told them that he had made a profit of Rs 10,000.

Jadiya Devi, his mother, and Durga, his wife, both had the same reaction—advising Ramkrishna to exercise prudence. The fact that he had stolen Durga's jewellery did not even enter the discussion.

Jadiya Devi counselled her son to square up the deal immediately. 'If you think about it, the interest on investing the ten thousand rupees will be over Rs 50 per month. That is enough for us, Ramkrishna. There is no need for you to take such risks. And anyway, only money earned through honest labour brings true satisfaction,' she said.

Durga too advised caution in all dealings. 'You come from a good family. Your father was a saintly man. Even though your great-grandfather was rich, and your father saw those prosperous times, once the money was given away in charity, your father remained true to the teachings he had learnt,' Durga said wisely.

Ramkrishna felt lighter after sharing the burden he had been carrying. However, he could not control his speculative urges.

Due to his various purchases, the profit on his initial investment had soared to Rs 75,000. While part of him wanted to continue speculating, another part recalled his mother's advice. He was in a quandary, doubts crept in about what would happen if the market trend reversed and prices started going south.

Amid these conflicting thoughts, he decided to visit his uncle. Ramkrishna's grandfather and his uncle's father had been brothers. His uncle was considered by the family and community to be a well-to-do man with a flourishing business. However, Ramkrishna was surprised to find that his uncle's office was a small room, barely five feet by five feet.

After they sat down in the small room, his uncle enquired after Ramkrishna's family. Once the small talk was over, his uncle asked Ramkrishna why he had come to see him. Ramkrishna sensed that his uncle was apprehensive, perhaps expecting to be asked for a loan. As everyone knew, Ramkrishna was hard up for cash, he thought his uncle's apprehension was valid.

With restrained glee, Ramkrishna told his uncle that he had made a profit of Rs 50,000 from some business deals. Even now, Ramkrishna hesitated to disclose the full extent of the profit that could be made in the silver trade.

His uncle was stunned. At first, he could not believe what Ramkrishna was saying. However, after several attempts, Ramkrishna managed to convince him.

'Arrey beta, you're talking of Rs 50,000? You know that today, even Rs 10,000 is enough for a person to never work again in his life and still keep his family in great comfort,' he exclaimed.

'I know, Uncle,' Ramkrishna replied, 'but I want to continue the business to make even more money.'

'Beta, you know that the local community does not think well of you. They say that you are always asking them for money, and when some do lend you the money, you are unable to pay them back. Speculation is a fickle business. It may bring you money, but it will never bring you respect. My advice is not to be greedy,' said his uncle.

Ramkrishna folded his hands and thanked his uncle for the advice. As he got up to leave, his uncle added, 'By the way, beta, if you are looking to invest part of your profit in any business, I will be happy if you considered mine. After all, why look outside the family?'

Ramkrishna nodded and promised his uncle he would keep that in mind. However, as he left the office, Ramkrishna smiled to himself. *This is the same man who wouldn't even loan me five rupees when I desperately needed it. And now he expects me to invest in his business!* he thought. But then, he checked himself, remembering his mother's advice to never be arrogant in dealings with people.

Lady Luck Finally Smiles on Ramkrishna

Ramkrishna had been working with very wealthy people since his adolescence. He had seen large sums of money pass through his hands, but it had never been his own money. He yearned for the thrill of having wealth he could call his own. He was ambitious and somewhat cocky about his prowess as a speculator.

He took a novel route to the deal. He instructed one of his agents in London to square up the trade—which meant selling all the silver he had bought. This would generate his Rs 75,000 in profit. However, being the speculator that he was, he instructed another agent to buy an equal amount of silver as he was selling through the first agent. His reasoning was that this approach would secure the profits from settling the trade, and if the market fluctuated, he would lose only a small amount. If the market remained steady, all he would have to pay would be the commission on the trade.

Ramkrishna went about his daily routine in a state of bliss. He believed that Goddess Lakshmi had truly smiled on him. Yet, those around him were unaware of his newfound success. He was still treated as an unreliable defaulter in the local community.

Destiny was enjoying playing with Ramkrishna. As luck would have it, the cable he had sent the first agent to sell the silver and settle the trade was garbled during transmission. The agent sent word that he could not understand the instructions and asked Ramkrishna to resend the cable.

This essentially meant that Ramkrishna, without meaning to, had doubled the amount of his trade. No sale had taken place; instead, an equivalent amount had been bought and the financial risk had also doubled.

By the time Ramkrishna got the first agent's cable asking for clear instructions, the market had moved again. Thankfully, it had moved up.

Ramkrishna lost no time in sending clear instructions to both agents to sell immediately and square up the trade deals. By this time, his profit was over Rs 1,56,000. This was a sum beyond Ramkrishna's wildest dreams. However, he could not share the news with anyone yet. (In today's terms, this amount would be equivalent to more than a few tens of crore rupees.)

Although Ramkrishna could write and speak English, he was not proficient in it. Anxious to secure the money, he sent a cablegram with a simple message: 'Send Money'.

The agents transferred the money to three different banks in Calcutta. Since Ramkrishna did not previously have a bank account, he had to open three separate accounts, which he promptly did.

With the money in his accounts, Ramkrishna was thrilled and felt rich. He revelled in the feeling. Feeling magnanimous, he wanted to share the joy of his newfound wealth. He decided to start with the munshi of one of the banks where he had opened an account. Munshis were typically employed by banks to report on the financial positions of businessmen. Ramkrishna had befriended this munshi, who had given favourable references about him to the agents in London. Ramkrishna felt indebted to him, knowing that no agent in London would have touched him had they sought references from the local merchants or traders in his community.

Ramkrishna knew that the munshi was a proud man and would not accept money from him outright. He also knew that he was a man of modest means and was accustomed to receiving baksheesh of two or at most five rupees from businessmen.

However, Ramkrishna wanted to give him Rs 5,000. To avoid it being perceived as a bribe, Ramkrishna told the munshi he wanted to invest in his private business shop. When the munshi hesitated, Ramkrishna told him to consider the money as a loan that he could repay later. Years later, Ramkrishna told the munshi to keep the money as his own.

From the bank Ramkrishna went straight to the silver market. He walked with a confident swagger, a big smile on his face. However, people in the market averted their eyes when they saw Ramkrishna. No one knew about his profits from the silver trade. To them, he was still a defaulter with no money. No one wanted to speak with him, let alone do business.

Ramkrishna realized this. He wanted to see the expressions on their faces when they found out that he was now richer than all of them. He tried to catch their eyes, but no one was willing to acknowledge him.

Ramkrishna, then, walked to the middle of the market and clapped his hands a few times to draw attention. Even though people did not want to acknowledge him, they were curious about what he was up to.

'Listen, everyone, listen!' Ramkrishna shouted at the top of his voice.

'Anyone who has lent me money can come to me right now, and I will repay them in full,' he declared.

A murmur spread through the gathered crowd. Ramkrishna was offering to clear all his debts? The traders exchanged puzzled looks and shook their heads in disbelief.

'Poor man, he must have lost his mind, unable to bear the burden of his misfortune,' tut-tutted one trader to another.

Another trader laughed loudly as he watched Ramkrishna standing in the middle of the market. 'He thinks we will believe him? This must be a trick to borrow more money from us,' he said to his neighbour, who scratched his head in bewilderment.

Ramkrishna waited for someone to approach him, but no one did. It was his turn to feel puzzled.

'Don't you people want your money back? I owe a total of Rs 30,000 to various people in this market. Come and take your money,' Ramkrishna called out loudly.

The gathered traders were stunned. Then, they began to laugh. They pointed at Ramkrishna and mocked him. No one took him seriously. They could not believe that a man who had been a defaulter for so long, shunned by the local community, could suddenly come into money without them even knowing about it.

Ramkrishna stood watching everyone around him. He was offended by the way people were treating him, but he knew he had no choice. He was a defaulter, and he had to first clear his debts. He did not like being made to feel small, with people sniggering and mocking him. He also felt powerless. A part of him knew that if those laughing at him were aware of the extent of his wealth, they would stop immediately. Yet, a perverse part of him wanted to see how far they would go.

As he stood waiting for people to stop laughing and talking among themselves about him, Ramkrishna saw a trader hurrying towards the gathered crowd. It was Seth Harzirimal Somany, almost running as he clutched the end of his dhoti in one hand and his umbrella in the other.

Seth Somany arrived and announced that he had checked with a bank manager who confirmed that Ramkrishna had indeed come into great wealth. The money had come from London, and there was a significant sum in Ramkrishna's account.

A hush fell over the gathered people. Then, like a pack of vultures, they pounced on Ramkrishna. His creditors shouted out the amounts he owed them, demanding immediate repayment. People pulled at his kurta to get his attention, shoving and pushing one another as Ramkrishna stood silently in the middle of it all. He did not bother to verify the amounts being claimed and simply paid whatever was demanded. By the end of the day, Ramkrishna was debt free.

Ramkrishna returned home, both exhausted and exhilarated. Word had spread, and the family knew something significant had happened. They were waiting eagerly for Ramkrishna's arrival. As soon as he entered, he went straight to his sleeping daughter. He picked her up, hugged her and kissed her forehead, remembering what Pandit Motiram had told him—that Lakshmi had come into their home.

Ramkrishna believed that Rama had brought him luck. He told the family about his newfound wealth. It took them a few moments to fully comprehend the enormity of it all.

Later, Jadiya Devi had a quiet word with her son. 'Your father once worked for my brother, Ramkrishna. Even you did at one time. Those were difficult times, and my brother lent us money. Though he has never asked for it back, the debt is a burden that weighs heavily on me. I want you to return the loan to your uncle,' she said.

The very next day, Ramkrishna went to meet his uncle, who had already heard about his nephew's newfound riches. When Ramkrishna told him he had come to repay his father's debt, his uncle was overcome with emotion. The incident of Ramkrishna sharing the silver prices with other traders was forgotten. He hugged Ramkrishna affectionately and declared that henceforth, no son of his would get married without the presence of Ramkrishna's entire family. It was another moment of wry reflection for Ramkrishna as he remembered how this same uncle had refused to meet him during the past few years.

And so it continued. As news of Ramkrishna's wealth spread, people began visiting him from far and wide. Many claimed to be long-lost or distant relatives. Some said they had known his father, while others claimed they were from the same village as the Dalmias. Yet, they all had one thing in common—they wanted money from Ramkrishna.

Ramkrishna found it ironic that people who would not even meet his eyes in fear of being asked for a loan were now eager to speak with him. He realized this was because he was now rich. He asked himself what it truly meant to be rich. Was it having a large bank balance? Was it controlling a big business empire? After much internal debate, Ramkrishna concluded that a wealthy man was one with a large heart, full of human kindness, one who placed his faith in God rather than in material wealth and one who remembered the virtues of piety, generosity and charity.

This period taught Ramkrishna valuable lessons that stayed with him throughout his life.

Ramkrishna was a speculator, but the speculation in the market about the source of his sudden wealth was rampant. Over a lakh of rupees was no trivial sum, and people could not fathom where the money had come from. Some said that Ramkrishna had won the Derby sweep; others claimed that he had found an ancient treasure of gold sovereigns in a field. Still others averred he had earned the money through gambling.

It was common to see groups of traders in the local market sipping tea and discussing how Ramkrishna had come into his wealth. The stories got wilder and wilder.

Ramkrishna ignored all the gossip and focused on clearing his debts. After paying off every penny he owed, Ramkrishna was left with over Rs 1 lakh. In 1917, this sum was an extraordinarily large amount of money. From paupers, the family had become immensely wealthy.

However, there was one debt that still needed to be repaid.

One morning, after his usual dip in the river, Ramkrishna went to Pandit Motiram's home. The astrologer was surprised to see him. He, too, knew of Ramkrishna's success in the silver trade. Pandit Motiram thought that Ramkrishna had come to gloat over the fact that the astrologer had lost out on a share of the profits as he had cancelled the silver trade deal. But he was pleasantly surprised when Ramkrishna bowed down and touched his feet.

'It is because of you and the cancelled deal that I have come into all this money, Panditji. Had you not backed out I would have made just a few hundred rupees in commission. But now, look—I have made over a lakh. I wanted to thank you and offer a token of my appreciation,' Ramkrishna said.

With that, he handed the astrologer Rs 5,000.

In Ramkrishna's mind, he had cleared all his debts, and it was now time to do more business.

6

Speculating in Silver and Becoming Wealthy

RAMKRISHNA moved his family to a bigger house after his windfall from the silver trade. He did not want them to live in cramped circumstances. However, their lifestyle did not change much. There was no ostentatious display of wealth. Jadiya Devi ensured that the riches did not go to any of her children's heads.

Durga's health had been delicate since the birth of Rama. She needed rest, and Jadiya Devi looked after her. It became apparent that Durga would not be able to bear any more children in the future.

Meanwhile, Ramkrishna continued doing what he knew best—speculating on the market. As any speculator knows, volatility is part of the game. Times can be good one moment and bad the next. It is a very rare speculator who can consistently beat the market. Ramkrishna was a good speculator, but he was not one of those rare few. Thus, he won some deals while losing others.

Despite earning substantial profits initially, within a year, Ramkrishna had lost it all. He had started small after losing his job with his uncle, but the addiction to speculation had taken hold of him. He had also experienced the power of money. After making his fantastic profit from the silver deal, he saw that people's behaviour towards him changed. They were no longer dismissive, nor did they try to avoid him. More and more people wanted to do business with him.

However, one thing continued to rankle—he still did not receive the respect he longed for. He told himself that it was just a matter of time. He believed that respect was given to those with money and waited for his wealth to start working its magic, bringing him the kind of respect his great-grandfather had enjoyed.

Money, however, seemed to have a mind of its own. Ramkrishna speculated heavily in the Calcutta satta bazaar and lost everything he had earned.

Once again, Ramkrishna became penniless. But this time there was a difference in the attitude of people towards him. He found that his name was worthy of credit in the market. Everyone remembered that Ramkrishna had paid back every single person he owed when he had come into money. Moreover, they saw that he was not vindictive with those who had treated him badly. In fact, he went out of his way to treat people better when he had the money. Thus, while Ramkrishna did not get the respect he craved, he did get people's affection.

This was around the time the First World War was drawing to a close. The market remained volatile, and Ramkrishna knew he lacked the financial heft to deal in large quantities of silver. Nevertheless, he realized it was a good time to trade in the metal. Once the war ended and stability returned, the opportunities to make quick money through speculation would diminish. He wanted to take advantage of the market's volatility.

He decided to speak to his maternal uncle, who had remained affectionate towards him, particularly after Ramkrishna had become rich. Ramkrishna, too, did not bear any grudges. He recognized his uncle's seniority and extensive network in the market.

'Uncle, I have a business idea. I think you'll find it interesting,' said Ramkrishna after greeting his uncle with folded hands.

'What is the idea now, Ramkrishna? You are always full of ideas,' said Motilal affectionately as he returned the greeting and then gestured for Ramkrishna to take a seat.

'I want to form a syndicate to buy silver. There is a huge opportunity in the market, but I do not have the money needed to leverage it,' Ramkrishna explained eagerly, leaning forward in his chair.

'Tell me more, Ramkrishna.' Motilal was interested. He knew his nephew had a sharp mind.

'Uncle, as you know, a syndicate is a temporary alliance of individuals, or even businesses, that come together to manage a large transaction that would be difficult to carry out individually. I want to buy a significant amount of silver because I'm sure the price will rise substantially in a short period of time. Look around you, don't you see a huge opportunity?' Ramkrishna said, throwing his arms wide and looking around animatedly.

'So, you're sure that silver prices will go up and you want to buy. What do you need from me? You do know that I don't have the kind of money you may require,' Motilal said thoughtfully, weighing his nephew's words. He saw the opportunity but knew such an enterprise would need a significant amount of capital.

'Yes, yes, Uncle I know that,' Ramkrishna said eagerly, pleased that his uncle was interested.

'See, Uncle, you have a larger credit limit in the market. My credit is limited because of my recent losses. Let's bring in other traders who will contribute the required money. Plus, another advantage of forming a syndicate is that the risk will be spread across all the members,' Ramkrishna explained, outlining his plan.

'Ah, I understand now, Ramkrishna. Very well, I'm open to the idea. Let's move ahead with it together,' Motilal said briskly. Now that he had made up his mind, he wanted to get the idea going.

'But, Uncle, I have one condition,' Ramkrishna interjected.

'Now what, my nephew?' Motilal asked with mild exasperation, slapping his forehead.

'Nothing much, Uncle. The condition is that I will be in charge of all decisions,' Ramkrishna said firmly.

Motilal saw no harm in the proposal. In fact, he saw only benefits. He knew his nephew and was confident the venture would be fruitful. He agreed and told Ramkrishna to proceed with the plan.

A year ago, it would have been almost impossible for Ramkrishna to get anyone to listen to him about an investment opportunity. But such is the power of money that now, wealthy businessmen in the market gave him a patient hearing. Soon, he was able to bring a few influential investors into the syndicate.

Once the syndicate was formed, Ramkrishna got to work. They quickly managed to corner almost all the silver available in the country, purchasing it on credit. The plan was to sell the stock once the prices went up. Even after covering the initial purchase cost and paying a small commission, the syndicate members would make a handsome profit. The silver they had bought was worth several crores, but they did not have to pay the entire amount upfront. They only had to pay the margin money.

As they waited for the silver market to move, Ramkrishna needed about Rs 1 crore to cover their short-term position. After pooling resources from all the syndicate members, they still fell short by Rs 15 lakh. Desperate, Ramkrishna tried to mortgage the silver stock and even agreed to pay a usurious interest rate of 12 per cent per month. Despite his efforts, he could not find the money to cover the shortfall.

Uncle and nephew were now very worried. The entire plan could collapse for want of Rs 15 lakh.

Ramkrishna was disheartened. He knew in his bones that silver prices would rise and that the syndicate would make a large profit. However, he was at a loss as to how to raise the necessary funds. He decided to discuss the situation with his uncle. Before leaving home, he went to see his daughter Rama, who was playing in her room. He kissed her on the forehead and then left the house.

As Motilal and Ramkrishna settled down to deliberate, a staff member brought cold *chaas* and snacks for them.

'What can we do now, Ramkrishna?' Motilal asked as he bit into a samosa. He closed his eyes as the hot potato filling burned his mouth.

Speculating in Silver and Becoming Wealthy

'Uncle, we cannot let the entire plan fail for just fifteen lakh rupees. We have to—no, we must—find a way to raise this amount,' Ramkrishna replied, breaking off a piece of his samosa and waiting for the filling to cool before putting it into his mouth.

The two men went over various ways to secure the funds. The staff kept replenishing their glasses, but Motilal put an end to the samosas.

'I can't have more than two samosas, bhai. Don't tempt me with more,' Motilal gently admonished his peon as he waved away the plate being set before them.

Suddenly, the phone on Motilal's desk rang. He picked it up and listened to the person on the other end of the line, who had a message for Ramkrishna.

'One Sir Narcat Warren wants you to go and meet him. Who is he, Ramkrishna?' said Motilal after he hung up, looking at his nephew quizzically.

'Oh, Sir Warren? He is the manager of the Bank of Bengal. I wonder why he wants to see me,' Ramkrishna mused, his face screwed up in thought.

'I think it would be better if you took someone along with you, beta,' Motilal advised.

Ramkrishna took a friend who was also a member of the syndicate. Together, they walked over to the bank.

'We are here to meet Sir Narcat Warren,' Ramkrishna said confidently to the officer at the front desk.

The officer, knowing Ramkrishna's reputation and that he had fallen on hard times again, decided to throw his weight around a bit.

'You know Warren sahib is a big man. How can you just come here and tell me to let you meet him?' the officer said brusquely.

'Arrey baba, he has asked us to meet him,' Ramkrishna replied reasonably, glancing at his friend for confirmation. His friend nodded eagerly at the officer.

'I don't believe you. Why would a big man want to meet a speculator, a gambler like you?' the officer continued, his tone offensive.

'Just go and tell him, please,' said Ramkrishna in a measured tone, laced with a hint of assertion. He was irritated by the officer's manner and especially by the allusion to him being a gambler, but he kept his emotions in check.

The officer went inside and returned with a sheepish expression.

'Okay, okay, come in. Warren sahib will see you now,' he said quickly, ushering them in without meeting their eyes.

Sir Narcat Warren sat in an impressive wood-panelled office with thick carpets. He did not get up to receive the two men but merely looked at them.

'Warren sahib, you wanted to see me?' Ramkrishna asked after greeting the manager.

'Oh yes, indeed, Ramkrishna. They tell me in the market that you are dealing in silver. Is that right?' Warren asked, leaning back into his chair and looking at the two men standing before him. He did not offer them a seat.

'Yes, sir, I do trade in silver,' Ramkrishna replied firmly, hiding his apprehension.

'Right, right. So, tell me, young man, how much silver do you have now?' Warren asked, leaning forward as if eager to get the answer.

Before Ramkrishna could reply, his friend tugged urgently at his sleeve. Ramkrishna looked at him with raised eyebrows. His friend gestured that he wanted to speak with him immediately.

Warren, who was observing the drama being played out in front of him with amusement, gestured for Ramkrishna to go outside and speak to his friend.

Once outside, Ramkrishna found his friend ashen-faced.

'I knew it, Ramkrishna, I knew it!' he cried, pulling out a handkerchief to wipe the sweat off his forehead.

'What did you know?' asked Ramkrishna, perplexed and slightly irritated. He wanted to return quickly so he could get to the bottom of the business of Warren summoning him.

'What you're doing is not right, Ramkrishna. They know we're holding a lot of silver. Now I will also get into trouble. Oh God, why did I agree to this stupid syndicate of yours?' his friend wailed, twisting his moist handkerchief into knots.

Ramkrishna understood his friend's concerns and patted him on the back.

'No one will say anything to you. You won't get into any trouble, I promise you. Just keep your cool,' Ramkrishna reassured him as he tugged the knotted handkerchief from his friend's grasp and slipped it into his pocket.

'But I'm with you! How can I not get into trouble? Warren knows that we're in this together. Oh, why did I come?' he wailed again, wringing his hands in despair. His handkerchief was in Ramkrishna's pocket and the friend was back to wringing his hands.

'Listen, now. Stop this *naatak* immediately. We'll go back inside, and I will do all the talking. I will tell him that you are my banker and have no idea about my business. Is that clear?'

Ramkrishna said firmly. The last thing he wanted was his friend saying something out of turn, leading to even more drama.

The friend nodded miserably.

'Come on now, smile. Don't look so woebegone. Smile, and remember—keep your mouth shut,' said Ramkrishna.

The two men returned to Warren's office, who looked up with a knowing smile. This time he offered them a seat across the table from him.

'So, are you ready to tell me how much silver you have?' he asked.

Before Ramkrishna could answer, his friend spoke. 'Warren sahib, I am just Ramkrishna's banker. I have no knowledge about the silver-vilver. Only he knows, and all of it belongs to him. I don't own any of it,' he said in a rush, completely forgetting Ramkrishna's instructions.

'I am least concerned about who owns the silver, young man,' said Warren, turning his attention back to Ramkrishna. 'All I want to know is how much you can sell now and at what price,' he added.

Ramkrishna heaved a mental sigh of relief. He was thankful that the ownership of the silver was not an issue. In fact, he saw a brilliant opportunity before him. Quickly doing some rough mental calculations, he provided the figures to Warren.

'Thank you. Let me check, and I will get back to you shortly,' said Warren as he made some notes on his notepad. Warren did not look up, and Ramkrishna took this as a signal for them to leave.

The two men walked out of the bank with mixed emotions. The friend was thanking his stars that he hadn't gotten into trouble. Ramkrishna, on the other hand, felt a twinge of excitement. Though he kept his emotions in check, he knew his

Speculating in Silver and Becoming Wealthy

problem had been solved. What he did not know was whether it had been solved fully or only partially.

The following day, there was another message from Sir Warren. This time, Ramkrishna went alone to meet him. Narcat Warren informed him that he had received a telegram from the government confirming their acceptance of the silver deal. The government was ready to buy the quantity of silver Ramkrishna had quoted, at the price he had specified.

Ramkrishna walked back to his uncle's office as if walking on air. The syndicate had made a very large profit. Even though Ramkrishna held only a 15 per cent share in the syndicate, he made several lakhs from the transaction.

He was back in the reckoning.

After the government bought all the silver from Ramkrishna and his syndicate, there was a lull in the market for a while. However, Ramkrishna, Motilal and the syndicate hoarded silver once again. And once more, the government bought it all.

By now, Ramkrishna had become a very wealthy man. The days of poverty were forgotten, not only by him but also by the market and the trader community. When Ramkrishna went to the local trader market, he was hailed by everyone, and people walked up to him to wish him. He was now addressed as 'Seth'—a mark of respect and a title accorded to the wealthy. From Ramkrishna, he had become Seth Ramkrishnaji.

Once he had regained his wealth, Ramkrishna wanted to settle all the debts he had incurred during the preceding years. During the lean period after his earlier profits from the silver trade had been speculated away, he had borrowed money from several people in the market. Those debts were weighing heavily on him. Although he was a speculator, Ramkrishna was honest at heart and had been brought up with strong family values. He wanted to return the money to his lenders, which he now did with ease.

One of the people he returned money to was Brij Rai Harsukh Rai. He had forgotten that he owed Harsukh Rai the last time he had settled all his debts. He wanted to rectify the oversight.

Ramkrishna's father had worked for Harsukh Rai at a salary of Rs 60 per month. Harsukh Rai had trusted Harjimal completely and would even leave the cash box in his custody. Ramkrishna used to visit his father at the office. This was the time when he himself was working with his maternal uncle. After work, he liked going to the riverbank to sit and watch the flowing water. It calmed him.

At the time, Ramkrishna wanted a bicycle. A bicycle was not cheap, and owning one in the early 1900s was a big deal. He asked his father for the money to buy one. However, his father explained that his salary was needed for household expenses and to send money back to Chirawa. Ramkrishna was disheartened, but the desire for a bicycle burnt bright within him.

One evening, when Ramkrishna went to his father's office, he found the room empty. A procession was passing through the lane, and the entire staff, including his father, had gone to see the tamasha. Drums resounded, conches blared and people danced on the road. In all probability, it was a wedding procession.

Ramkrishna found himself alone in the office. His eyes fell on the bunch of keys that his father, in his hurry, had left near his seat. Ramkrishna lost no time in taking the keys and trying each to see which opened the cash box. The fourth key he tried unlocked it. Inside, he saw bundles of loose cash. He took out a fistful of notes and stuffed them into his pocket. He quickly locked the cash box and left the keys in the same spot where he had found them.

He realized that no one had seen him enter the office, as everyone was busy watching the procession. Quietly, he slipped out and went home. No one saw him leave the office either.

Once home, he went to the bathroom and locked himself inside. When he counted the notes, he realized he had taken almost Rs 500 from the cash box—a large sum of money at the time. He used the money to buy a bicycle and, in a fit of extravagance, bought himself some gold buttons as well.

Back at the office, it was soon discovered that a large sum of money was missing from the cash box. However, such was the reputation of Harjimal, and such was the trust that Harsukh Rai had in him, that the needle of suspicion never even pointed towards the employee. It was assumed that a thief had stolen the money. No one talked about it further.

Now that Ramkrishna was wealthy, this was the debt he wanted to repay. He went to Harsukh Rai's office to settle it.

As he walked into the office, a buzz went around that Seth Ramkrishna had come to the humble establishment of Harsukh Rai. The owner himself stood up as Ramkrishna entered his room.

'Why did you bother to come, Sethji? You could have called me, and I would have come to meet you,' said Harsukh Rai deferentially. Seth Ramkrishna was a big man in the market, and Harsukh Rai was honoured that such an important individual had come to his modest office.

'No, no. I had to come, as I have a debt to repay to you,' said Ramkrishna with a smile. Though he did not show it, he was delighted by the manner in which he was being treated.

'A debt? How can you, such a wealthy seth, be in debt to a small trader like me?' Harsukh Rai asked, genuinely puzzled.

'I am in debt—have been, in fact, ever since my father worked for you some years ago,' explained Ramkrishna.

'Your father? How is that even possible? Why would the father of one of the richest men in Calcutta work for me?' Harsukh Rai said, looked around at his staff, who were hovering nearby. He looked flabbergasted, as though he thought Ramkrishna was joking or even mocking him.

Ramkrishna then told him the story of how he had taken money from the cash box. He took out Rs 1,000 from his pocket and handed it over to Harsukh Rai.

'Allow me to make amends for my mistake. I was a child and did not know what I was doing. I hope you can forgive me. And if you feel this amount is not enough, please let me know, and I will ensure the rest is sent to you,' Ramkrishna said.

Harsukh Rai was at a loss for words. He had forgotten about the missing Rs 500. Now, being repaid double that amount, he felt both surprised and happy.

He accepted the money with grace. In later years, when Ramkrishna's brother Jaidayal visited Calcutta, he would make it a point to visit Harsukh Rai. The Rai family was very proud of their association with the Dalmias.

Similarly, Ramkrishna returned the money to everyone he had borrowed from in the intervening year. Due to the wealth he had accumulated through the silver trade on the London Exchange, his credibility had increased significantly. Furthermore, people saw that Ramkrishna repaid all his debts, with interest, once he had the money. Thus, when he needed money for speculation, they were happy to lend it to him.

Speculating in Silver and Becoming Wealthy

Ramkrishna now faced a peculiar problem. After hoarding and selling silver to the government not once but twice, it appeared that all the silver had been sucked out of the market. Moreover, with the war having ended, speculative trading in silver had slowed down.

Ramkrishna grew restless. A speculator at heart, he wanted to continue trading. As silver was no longer an attractive option, he turned his attention to cotton.

He observed that while a large number of traders engaged in jute and cotton trading, the market itself was unstructured. He began speculating in these commodities and, in the process, discovered that traders had no proper place to conduct their business. They worked from under trees or makeshift seats along the roads. Ramkrishna wanted to change this.

He established the new Cotton Market in Calcutta and introduced a weekly or fortnightly payment system for the benefit of traders. He had heard that such a settlement cycle existed in the Liverpool Cottom Market in the UK and decided to implement it in Calcutta. This significantly decreased the risk for traders. Buyers and sellers faced no risk if the market prices rose or fell because their accounts were settled at the old rates in cash and new transactions took place afresh.

Around the same time Ramkrishna started speculating in cotton, he rented a large hall for Rs 500 per month and named it the Jute and Cotton Exchange Limited. While it was a limited company, Ramkrishna let it be believed that government permission had been obtained to set up the Exchange. He realized that many traders were ignorant and feared that as speculators, they could be arrested for gambling. Ramkrishna took advantage of their ignorance by implying that government permission had been acquired.

The large hall had several almirahs, each paired with a desk and chair. Ramkrishna allotted an almirah to each broker, who then installed a telephone. He charged every broker a monthly rent. The Exchange became popular in no time, and brokers vied with one another for space in the hall. Ramkrishna found that the rent proceeds alone amounted to Rs 10,000 per month. He deposited all the rental income into the accounts of the limited company.

Ramkrishna was in a happy state of mind. He was a well-known figure in Calcutta, and he had money in his name. People addressed him as 'Seth' or 'Sethji' instead of plain Ramkrishna. However, he continued to live and dress simply—in fact, austerely. While he did not object when the women in his family wanted to buy jewellery, he himself dressed in a simple khadi silk kurta and dhoti. Wealth did not change him as a person.

7

Ramkrishna's Guru and Mentor— Baldev Das Nathani

FOR the next fourteen years, Ramkrishna continued as a speculator-trader in the market. He conducted his business in both Calcutta and Bombay, dealing across various commodities and eventually also trading in shares.

There were times when he wanted to stop speculating, but it was like an addiction—he could not help himself and continued. There were times he made money, and at other times, he lost money.

Now that he was counted among the wealthy, even during his bleak periods, there was no dearth of people who wanted to associate with him. However, he noticed a subtle difference in the way people treated him compared to how they treated other businessmen who owned manufacturing factories. This puzzled him, as he believed he earned more money through speculation than they did from manufacturing.

Ramkrishna did consider setting up a factory, but he realized that his heart lay in speculation and trading in the market. It was this that brought him the greatest joy and kept his mind sharp. Understanding and analysing trends, joining the dots and then taking a call on the market required serious brain power, which Ramkrishna had, and he used it well.

Of course, there were times when the market behaved contrary to all analyses, and Ramkrishna lost money. However, he found it easy to borrow money whenever he needed it. He was known in the market as someone who always repaid his debts. In some cases, he even returned money to the descendants of people who had lent it to him. Often, these descendants had no idea their fathers had lent him money and saw the repayment as an unexpected windfall.

It was around this time that Ramkrishna met Baldev Das Nathani, a self-made man who had earned an impressive reputation in the Calcutta market. Though formally uneducated, Baldev Das was one of the wealthiest men in the city. He had a saintly disposition and was known to all as a compassionate and forgiving individual.

During one of his lean periods, Ramkrishna had gone to meet Baldev Das. The older man had heard about Ramkrishna from the others in the market, and when he met him in person, he took an instant liking to young Ramkrishna. Maybe Baldev Das saw a bit of himself in the young man, as he too had been poor, earning only Rs 25 per month while working for his maternal uncle. Or maybe he recognized the business brilliance in Ramkrishna and sensed that the fatherless young man needed some parental guidance. Whatever the reason, he decided to help Ramkrishna.

Baldev Das inducted Ramkrishna into his brokerage firm, which was a partnership dealing exclusively in shares and stocks. Since Ramkrishna had a passion for commodity trading, Baldev Das allowed him to continue his other business interests outside the partnership.

'You can do business in my name, Ramkrishna. I will give you a 50 per cent share of whatever profit you make. If there is a loss, I will make the payment by debiting your account for the amount. This way, you don't need to worry about liquidity,' Baldev Das told Ramkrishna.

Ramkrishna was, of course, delighted and thanked the older man.

'Ramkrishna, today, you are going through a lean patch. Still, I am taking you on as my partner. There is only one thing I ask of you—do not deceive me,' Baldev Das cautioned him.

Baldev Das continued to shower his attention, love and affection on the young Ramkrishna, who came to view Baldev Das as a surrogate father and considered him as his guru. He often visited his mentor to seek his advice and soon earned Baldev Das's trust and enjoyed his full confidence. Ramkrishna's life and outlook were greatly influenced by Baldev Das.

For his part, the older man saw Ramkrishna as a son and often shared stories from his own life and the lessons he had learnt. He appreciated Ramkrishna's sharp intelligence and shrewd mind. However, whenever Ramkrishna discussed the possibility of setting up a factory, Baldev Das would discourage him.

'You have a sharp mind, Ramkrishna. Utilize your intelligence and energy in the market only. You will earn good dividends from this,' he said one evening after the trading hours. Both men were sitting together companionably after a hectic day of trading. Baldev Das sipped his tea as he looked at Ramkrishna keenly.

'But Bare Babuji, I want both money and respect,' Ramkrishna replied, almost childlike. He found that he could talk about his deepest fears and desires with the older man, whom he addressed as Bare Babuji.

'Ah, respect! Begin by earning money and keeping it instead of speculating it away. Money will enable you to wear a chain of diamonds and gems, keep as many servants as you like and buy as many motor cars as you want. After that, you can chase respect,' said Baldev Das with a knowing smile.

Baldev Das was a share broker and understood the stock market better than the commodity market. Periodically, he would urge Ramkrishna to focus more on the share market.

'You are allowing your attention to be diverted by engaging in the cotton and jute business, my boy,' Baldev Das advised Ramkrishna. 'Focus on the share market, and you will earn more money,' he added.

However, Ramkrishna enjoyed dealing in commodities. Whenever he tried to counter his mentor's advice, Baldev Das would respond with sound reasoning and a sop.

'You know, Ramkrishna, commodity brokers give 15 annas (one rupee had 16 annas) on profits but take 17 annas on losses. On top of that, you have to worry about arranging finance for the trades. However, in the share market, if you suffer a loss, I will pay it, and you won't have to worry about it at all,' he told Ramkrishna. Share trading done by Ramkrishna under the firm's name would be a firm responsibility, and thus, Ramkrishna would not be personally liable for any losses.

Baldev Das knew Ramkrishna well. He understood that the addiction and excitement of commodity speculation overtook the young man's sanity at times. So, he counselled his mentee not to do any business without his knowledge.

But Ramkrishna was Ramkrishna. He could not help himself and would surrender to the temptation of speculating, acting against the advice of his mentor. Yet, such was Baldev Das's temperament that he would never get angry.

On one occasion, Ramkrishna engaged in a speculative deal in cotton and incurred a loss of Rs 30,000. He was already in debt to Baldev Das for more than Rs 1,50,000. He needed more money to cover his losses. Although Baldev Das had told him not to speculate in commodities, he had ignored his cautionary advice again. Yet, he needed the money, and so he went to Baldev Das's office.

Baldev Das used to sit on the first floor of the office building. Normally, visitors were screened on the ground floor, and access to the first floor was controlled by the staff. However, Ramkrishna was a well-known face, and everyone was aware of the special relationship he had with Baldev Das. Thus, he walked into the building and went straight to the first floor.

He told Baldev Das that he needed money.

'How much do you need, Ramkrishna?' asked Baldev Das, looking up from the papers he was studying. He adjusted his spectacles to get a better look at Ramkrishna.

'Bare Babuji, I need Rs 30,000,' answered Ramkrishna in a small voice. He could not look at Baldev Das directly and appeared sheepish.

'Arrey bhagwan, you've been speculating again? What is it this time? Cotton or jute?' exclaimed Baldev Das, striking his forehead with his hand. He sounded more irritated than angry.

'Bare Babuji, it's cotton. I did a deal, and I need to square off the losses. I thought it was a good deal, but …' Ramkrishna trailed off as Baldev Das looked at him sternly.

Shaking his head, Baldev Das looked knowingly at Ramkrishna from above his spectacles, which were sitting on his nose. And then he turned to his munshi and instructed him to issue a cheque for Rs 30,000 to Ramkrishna.

'Make sure you square up the trade, Ramkrishna. Settle the loss at this amount only,' Baldev Das cautioned once again, unsure if his protégé would heed his advice.

Ramkrishna took the cheque, thanked Baldev Das, and went to the market. Once there, he felt the buzz and was convinced the market was on its way up. He did not square the deal; instead, he used the money given by Baldev Das to trade more.

Unfortunately, the market went down even further. His total loss now stood at Rs 60,000. Ramkrishna returned to Baldev Das for help.

'So, you didn't listen to me, eh? When will you learn, my boy?' asked Baldev Das, not expecting an answer. He knew he should not indulge Ramkrishna but couldn't help himself. He was very fond of him and knew the young man bore no malice towards anyone and never cheated anyone. Speculation was an addiction, and he needed to be weaned off it.

As expected, Ramkrishna said nothing.

'If you continue doing this, you will make me a pauper very soon. Or a defaulter at the very least,' Baldev Das said, trying some emotional blackmail.

Still, Ramkrishna remained silent.

'All right, I'll give you the money to cover this loss as well. But touch my feet and take an oath that you will not speculate privately again,' said Baldev Das.

Ramkrishna touched his mentor's feet and mumbled something.

Gambling, however, is an addictive habit, and it is difficult for a gambler to break free. Soon enough Ramkrishna speculated again, and this time, the loss went up to Rs 1 lakh. Ramkrishna found himself in a dilemma. How could he approach Baldev Das yet again? He knew he was at fault but couldn't stop himself from speculating.

He came up with a way around the problem. Instead of going to the first floor to meet Baldev Das, Ramkrishna went straight to the cashier, Chhannumal. He told the cashier to loan him shares of Kumarhatti Jute worth Rs 1 lakh. The cashier knew that Ramkrishna was the blue-eyed boy of his boss. He was surprised when Ramkrishna told him to keep the transaction between them and not inform Baldev Das, but he agreed and kept the loan confidential.

Ramkrishna went to the market and sold off the shares to cover the Rs 1 lakh loss. Luckily for him, the market trend changed the following week, and he made a significant profit on his commodity trade. He used part of the profit to buy back the Kumarhatti Jute shares and returned them to Chhannumal.

Ramkrishna tried to stop himself from further speculation but was a prisoner of his addiction. As night follows day, he incurred another loss. He went again to Chhannumal and requested a loan of shares worth Rs 1 lakh. Since Ramkrishna had promptly returned the shares the previous time, the cashier saw no reason not to give him the shares again.

This time, however, there was no gain. Ramkrishna could not return the shares even after two weeks. He would visit the cashier regularly and request him not to inform Baldev Das. The cashier heeded Ramkrishna's request for some time, but eventually decided it was better to let his boss know. Chhannumal did not want any aspersions cast on his own honesty.

'I am very sorry, Sethji, but he returned the shares promptly the last time. I thought he would do the same again. I didn't realize he wouldn't be able to return them this time,' said Chhannumal, almost in tears. One lakh was a huge sum of money, and he was terrified of the consequences if Ramkrishna failed to repay it.

'Don't worry, Chhannumal, don't worry. I am not upset with you. You did what you thought was best. But don't let Ramkrishna know you've told me,' said Baldev Das as he stood up and patted the young cashier on the back. He wanted to reassure Chhannumal that he would not be held responsible for any loss.

'Why, Sethji? Why shouldn't I let him know? He told me the same thing—to not let you know. This keeping of secrets is what has landed me in this situation,' Chhannumal said, looking down with a woebegone expression.

'Because if he believes I don't know, he will try his utmost to return the shares as soon as he can. However, if he knows that I know, the pressure of keeping a secret will be off his chest,' explained Baldev Das patiently.

The cashier understood and nodded in agreement.

Ramkrishna continued to believe that Baldev Das did not know that Chhannumal had loaned him shares worth Rs 1 lakh. The cashier, on the other hand, kept imploring Ramkrishna to return the shares. Unfortunately, the market remained unfavourable, and Ramkrishna was unable to buy back the shares as profits continued to elude him.

Baldev Das often ran into Ramkrishna in the market, but neither through his words nor his actions did he let slip that he knew about the borrowed shares.

Ramkrishna may have been a speculator, but he was an honest man. The fact that he owed Baldev Das a large sum of money bothered him. He knew that if Baldev Das discovered the 'theft' of shares, he would be well within his rights to file a criminal case against Ramkrishna. Anyone else who had shares worth such a large amount taken away without their knowledge would have done so.

But most of all, Ramkrishna remembered Baldev Das's words when he had been inducted into the partnership. Baldev Das had told him never to break his trust or deceive him. The fact that he was, in a sense, deceiving his mentor gnawed at Ramkrishna.

He lost his appetite and could not sleep properly. He knew he couldn't unload the burden of his misdeeds on his mother, or his wife Durga, or even his brother Jaidayal, who was eleven years younger than him. He was in agony. His family sensed that something was amiss, but Ramkrishna would not talk to them about it.

Finally, when he could bear it no longer, he went to his friend Ram Lal Burman. He sat him down and told him everything, explaining how he had taken shares from Baldev Das without his knowledge.

'I don't have the courage to go to him and confess my misdeeds, Ram Lal. Please, you go and tell him what I have done,' Ramkrishna implored.

'But Sethji is a big man. I am just a small trader. I can't simply walk into his office and ask to see him,' said Ram Lal.

Like everyone else, he was in awe of Baldev Das and couldn't imagine confessing his friend's wrongdoing to the great man.

'You may have a point, Ram Lal. Here is what you can do. Go to his office and tell his staff that you are a friend of mine and that you want to meet Sethji. I am sure you will get an audience,' Ramkrishna suggested.

Ram Lal agreed and went to Baldev Das's office. As expected, he was stopped on the ground floor. However, once he took Ramkrishna's name, he was allowed to proceed to the first floor.

Baldev Das was perplexed upon seeing the young man who had come to meet him. He did not know him and knew that his staff would not allow a stranger to walk into his office.

He looked at Ram Lal keenly. *'Kaise aana hua? Kuch kaam tha kya?'* he asked.

'Sethji, I am a friend of Ramkrishna's, and he has asked me to meet you,' said Ram Lal in a rush, eager to unload the burden of his friend's message as quickly as possible.

As soon as Ram Lal took his friend's name, a slow smile spread across the older man's face.

'Oh, so you are Ramkrishna's friend, are you?' asked Baldev Das as he leaned back in his seat.

'Haanji, Sethji,' Ram Lal confirmed.

'Tell me, what can I do for you? Any friend of Ramkrishna's is a friend of mine,' said Baldev Das.

'Ramkrishna wanted me to speak to you about …' Ram Lal began hesitantly.

But before he could finish, Baldev Das cut him short.

'I will not speak to you or listen to anything concerning Ramkrishna. Ask him to come and see me himself. I will talk only to him,' said Baldev Das firmly.

Ram Lal beat a hasty retreat.

'Sethji says he wants you to go and talk to him yourself. He refused to even speak to me about you,' Ram Lal reported back to his friend.

'Was he angry? Did he look upset?' asked Ramkrishna anxiously, concerned about the mood of his mentor.

'Not at all. He was most gracious and offered me tea and samosas. Of course, I did not take any. I came back here as fast as I could, Ramkrishna. Now, you go and see him,' said Ram Lal expansively. Now that the meeting with Baldev Das was over, he recalled it with happiness as he could tell his friends that he had met the great man.

Ramkrishna, however, was nervous—very nervous. He knew he was in the wrong. The rational part of his mind told him that he would have to confess to Baldev Das sooner or later, but he just could not muster the courage.

Baldev Das was a mild-mannered man who rarely lost his temper. Yet his staff and officers trembled before him. If they committed a mistake, they knew their boss might get angry, yet they were unsure of how to handle such a situation. Had Baldev Das been prone to losing his temper often and giving his staff a tongue-lashing, they would have gotten used to it. It was the fear of an outburst—whether it came or not—that made people nervous.

And so, Ramkrishna was nervous. He could not confide in anyone else. At times, he felt like jumping into the river and committing suicide, but the thought of his family, especially his daughter Rama, always stopped him. Other times, he wished the earth would open up and swallow him whole, but again, the image of Rama in his mind cooled such thoughts.

Finally, summoning all his courage, Ramkrishna went to Baldev Das's office. As it happened, Baldev Das was walking out of the building just as Ramkrishna arrived. Ramkrishna saw him and almost turned to run away, but Baldev Das waved at him and he lost the chance to escape.

Baldev Das smiled and made small talk as he walked with Ramkrishna to his office on the first floor. As soon as the older man sat down, Ramkrishna began speaking. It was as though a dam had burst. Words poured out in torrents, as if he were desperate to cleanse himself of his guilt.

Baldev Das raised his hand, gesturing for Ramkrishna to stop.

'I can't understand a word you're saying, Ramkrishna. Stop blabbering,' said Baldev Das.

Suddenly, Ramkrishna was at a loss for words. He stood mutely before his mentor.

'I already know what you have done, Ramkrishna,' said Baldev Das firmly.

With that one sentence, it was as though a 100-kilo burden had been lifted from Ramkrishna's shoulders. He felt lighter; half of his fear was no more.

Ramkrishna truly respected Baldev Das and looked up to him. In the absence of a father figure, he thought of the older man as one. So the idea that he might fall in the eyes of his mentor had been gnawing at Ramkrishna. More than guilt over his misdeeds, it was the fact that he was not being honest with Baldev Das whenever they met in the market that caused him pain and worry.

'You already knew, Bare Babuji?' asked Ramkrishna in astonishment.

'Yes. What did you think, Ramkrishna? That you could do something without me finding out? Not at all,' said Baldev Das with a knowing smile.

As Ramkrishna started to apologize and explain himself, Baldev Das cut him short again.

'There is no doubt you have committed some very serious mistakes. But the real mistake is not what you think it is,' said Baldev Das, wagging his finger at Ramkrishna.

He asked Ramkrishna to sit down, then pointed towards the four walls of the room. Ramkrishna wondered what Baldev Das was doing.

'Ramkrishna, even walls have ears. If something reaches a third ear, it cannot remain a secret. You have told your friend. Now it will not be possible to keep your misdeeds a secret,' said Baldev Das softly, as if he, too, were cautious of the walls.

Ramkrishna reflected on these words and nodded slowly.

'Ramkrishna, I want you to sit at the same table as G.D. Birla—as an equal. You keep saying you want respect. Besides having money, associating with well-known and respected people also earns you respect. Thus, be very careful about what you say to others about your business affairs. Now that this matter is no longer private, I am worried about how it will reflect on you,' said Baldev Das.

As Ramkrishna hung his head in shame, Baldev Das stood up and walked over to him. He patted the young man on the back and told him to go home and get a good night's sleep.

'You look like you have not slept in a month, Ramkrishna,' he said with a laugh.

Ramkrishna looked up with gratitude, folded his hands and went home.

For the first time in many weeks, Ramkrishna slept soundly.

Baldev Das, in his inimitable style, handled the matter in such a manner that news of Ramkrishna's misdeeds did not become public. Such was the trust the older man reposed in the younger one that their relationship continued without even a flicker of strain.

Baldev Das was also responsible for teaching Ramkrishna more life lessons. However, he did not sit him down and deliver sermons. Instead, the lessons Ramkrishna learnt came through observation.

Bird and Company, a British firm in Calcutta, had a clerk who wanted to trade shares through Baldev Das's brokerage. The clerk deposited Rs 1,000 as margin money to purchase shares.

In the 1920s, margin buying—or purchasing shares by paying a small amount of money while the broker loaned the rest—was not regulated by the government. It was controlled by brokers, who were focused on their own interests and profits. Typically, the average margin needed was 50 per cent of the stock price. In the excitement of trading using only margin money, people often forgot that the leveraging exposed them to a greater downside risk than outright cash purchases as the margin loan had to be repaid even if the share values plummeted.

The price of the shares went up, and the clerk bought more shares with his profits. Again, he did not pay the full amount but only a fraction of the share price as he bought them on margin. As the market was on an upward trend, the clerk continued to buy more shares with his profits. However, then the market dropped, and the clerk was in serious debt. After selling all his shares at the lower price and accounting for the borrowed amount, he owed Rs 40,000.

One day, while sitting with the accountant and Baldev Das, Ramkrishna noticed the shortfall. He asked Baldev Das, 'Bare Babuji, why aren't you squaring up the trade? If there is a further loss, you will get nothing. There is still a chance to recover some of the money if the market goes up.'

Baldev Das looked at Ramkrishna and smiled fondly.

'Ramkrishna, I can square up the trade. But then this clerk would become my debtor. If he is unable to pay me back, he might be born as a donkey in his next life, or a horse, or worse—even a relative of mine! I don't want that to happen. I can wait,' said Baldev Das. He wanted to give the clerk a chance to repay.

As it often happens in the market, share prices rose again. The clerk was able to cash in his profits and pay back Baldev Das.

'That's one less relative of mine in my next birth!' said Baldev Das with a relieved laugh.

Baldev Das had formed a partnership with Ramkrishna for share trading and broking. While Ramkrishna was free to pursue his other business activities independently, the partnership activities were largely controlled by Baldev Das.

There came a time when Baldev Das himself was in serious financial trouble. The partnership had bought Kumarhatti shares, and the market had gone down. A share that had been trading at Rs 1,200 had fallen to Rs 475.

Ramkrishna thought that if he bought more shares at the lower price, he could stop its downward trajectory. However, he knew Baldev Das would not agree to the idea, as the partnership was already holding a large number of shares and faced large potential losses.

Ramkrishna wanted to help the partnership, and after some thought, he came up with an idea. He decided to buy Kumarhatti shares through his uncle Motilal's firm. He hoped that the large buy orders in the market would stop the share prices from falling. Ramkrishna planned that should there be a loss on the shares he bought, he would bear it personally. However, if there was a profit, he would use the gains to pay off the partnership's losses.

Everything was going fine—until it wasn't.

One of Motilal's cousins, Meghraj, was also part of the uncle's business. Although the deal with Kumarhatti shares was a private arrangement between Motilal and Ramkrishna, Meghraj somehow got wind of it. Meghraj, being risk-averse and not a speculator, became nervous about the deal. He tried speaking with Motilal, but the uncle did not want to discuss it.

As his anxiety grew, Meghraj took an unwarranted step. He issued a pamphlet in the market, warning traders to beware of fraudsters claiming to be doing business in the name of Motilal's firm. The pamphlet further declared that the firm would not be liable for any payments related to such trades.

The pamphlet, however, did not create even a ripple in the market. People dismissed it as a joke or the work of a jealous competitor. Seeing that it had no effect, Meghraj became even more nervous. Further, he had stuck his neck out and could not be seen to be backing down. When he saw that the market's attitude towards Ramkrishna did not change despite the wide distribution of the pamphlet, Meghraj decided to escalate matters.

He went directly to Baldev Das's office. He told the staff on the ground floor that he was Ramkrishna's relative and was granted an immediate audience with Baldev Das.

'Have you done any transaction in our name?' Meghraj came straight to the point, not bothering to greet the older man or attempt politeness.

'For what? What are you saying?' Baldev Das responded curtly. He did not like the attitude of the young man standing with arms akimbo before him.

'Has any transaction in Kumarhatti shares been done in our firm's name?' Meghraj repeated, this time speaking louder and enunciating each word as though Baldev Das were hard of hearing.

The sharp man that he was, Baldev Das immediately understood that Ramkrishna had done a deal through his uncle's firm. However, he was also angered by Meghraj's attempt to drive a wedge between him and Ramkrishna.

'Why have you come to my office? Do you want to ruin Ramkrishna's career and name? Isn't his mother like your sister? Why are you trying to sully the name of your sister's family?' Baldev Das fired these questions like bullets. Though he did not get angry very often, this time his temper flared.

Meghraj, unperturbed, persisted in demanding to know if there had been a deal.

'There is no such deal. Now leave,' said Baldev Das, making a shooing gesture with his hands. He then called his staff and told them to escort Meghraj out of the office.

News of Meghraj's visit and heated exchange with Baldev Das quickly spread and soon reached Ramkrishna's ears.

When Ramkrishna heard about the incident, he asked Baldev Das why he had lied about the trade. In his calm manner, Baldev Das replied, 'If someone has good intentions and tells a lie, then there is no sin in it.'

The matter, in any case, was resolved as the market trend reversed and it went up. There was an overall profit in Kumarhatti shares and no one was out of pocket.

In his later years, Ramkrishna often reflected on the days spent with Baldev Das and the lessons he had learnt merely by being with the older man and talking to him. These lessons became part of his subconscious and often surfaced whenever Ramkrishna was in a dilemma.

Ramkrishna had always seen Baldev Das as calm and composed. However, there were two occasions when the older man became emotional and had tears in his eyes.

One such instance involved Baldev Das's younger brother, Basant Lal. Even though Basant Lal was somewhat wayward, his elder brother had only affection for him. Basant Lal was also a partner in the firm, though he held a smaller share than Ramkrishna's 25 per cent.

Kumarhatti Jute shares were heavily traded in the Calcutta stock market. When a share is traded in large quantities, the opportunities for profit increase as liquidity is high. Basant Lal wanted to corner the market for these shares and, thus, potentially earn more profit. He repeatedly asked his elder brother to buy large quantities of the shares. Baldev Das did not want to and resisted his brother's entreaties most of the time.

However, on one occasion, Basant Lal was relentless in his pursuit of purchasing Kumarhatti Jute shares. Baldev Das eventually gave in to his brother's request and bought a large quantity through the firm. The market fell soon after the transaction.

Realizing the extent of the losses, Basant Lal wanted to sell the shares to cut the firm's losses. However, Baldev Das refused to allow the sale to proceed.

After repeated requests to his brother failed to have any effect, Basant Lal became desperate and stormed off to Ramkrishna's house.

Ramkrishna was flustered to see Baldev Das's brother in his house.

'Sethji, if you wanted to meet me, all you had to do was call. I would have dropped everything and come running to you,' said Ramkrishna as he hurried out to the courtyard to greet him.

Basant Lal brushed this aside with an impatient wave of his hand. He clearly had other things on his mind.

'Ramkrishna, my older brother wants to ruin me completely,' complained Basant Lal.

'No, no, no, Sethji, Bare Babuji is not like that. Why would he want to ruin you or let harm come to you? After all, you are his younger brother, and he loves you,' Ramkrishna quickly reassured him.

Noticing a member of the household staff hovering behind the door, Ramkrishna gestured for him to bring out a couple of cane chairs and some water for the visitor.

'Ramkrishna, you see him through rose-tinted glasses. You can't see any fault in what he does. But I can see clearly that he wants to ruin me financially,' said Basant Lal as he sank into a cane chair with a deep sigh. Accepting the glass of water, he took a large sip. His emotions were in turmoil, and the water helped him calm down.

'Will you tell me, Sethji, what exactly is the matter?' asked Ramkrishna, taking advantage of Basant Lal's apparent composure.

'He is not permitting me to sell my shares of Kumarhatti Jute,' Basant Lal erupted, losing his composure in a jiffy as he raised his voice and complained to Ramkrishna.

Ramkrishna tried to explain to Basant Lal that when shares were bought by the firm, they did not belong to any individual partner but to the firm as a whole. Thus, no partner could claim 'his share' of shares. Once the shares were sold, the profit or loss would go into the firm's account.

However, Basant Lal refused to understand and continued ranting about his impending financial ruin.

Ramkrishna listened patiently for as long as he could. When he could no longer bear to hear the litany of complaints against his mentor, he tried one final time to reason with him.

'Sethji, you and Bare Babuji live in the same house. The ground floor is the office, Bare Babuji lives on the first floor and you stay on the second floor, which is big, spacious and well-ventilated. Now, how can you even think that your brother wishes you harm?' Ramkrishna asked Basant Lal as he leaned forward and patted Basant Lal's arm.

'I don't know anything about all that. But you go and tell him this. See if you can convince him to sell the shares,' Basant Lal demanded, refusing to calm down.

Ramkrishna went to Baldev Das and relayed the conversation. Baldev Das heard him out calmly without interrupting. Once Ramkrishna finished, Baldev Das closed his eyes and tilted his face upwards as if appealing to the gods above.

'Ramkrishna, you know that Basant and I were both nourished in the same mother's womb. I love him more than I love my son, Rameshwar. Now that I have heard what has him so worried, I want you to convey a message to him from me,' said Baldev Das in a measured tone.

'Of course, Bare Babuji. What is the message?' Ramkrishna responded immediately.

'You go and tell him that he need not pay for any losses. However, if there is a profit, he will get his full share of it,' said Baldev Das.

'All right, Bare Babuji, I will tell Basant Lalji this. I hope it will put his mind at ease,' Ramkrishna said, getting up to leave. But Baldev Das gestured for him to stay a little longer.

'I hope so too, Ramkrishna, I hope so. And listen, you are also a four-anna share holder. You too will not bear any losses.'

'That is very gracious of you, Bare Babuji. Thank you, but there is no need for this,' said Ramkrishna, quite overwhelmed.

'There may be no need, but I must treat every partner in the firm equally. And I am not finished yet. When you talk to Basant, tell him I will credit Rs 10 lakh into his personal account,' Baldev Das continued.

Ramkrishna went to meet Basant Lal and conveyed Baldev Das's messages to him. Basant Lal's reaction surprised him.

'I will not beg in front of my brother. You go and tell that brother of mine this,' Basant Lal responded angrily to his elder brother's offer.

Ramkrishna was reluctant to convey this message to Baldev Das, knowing it would deeply hurt the older man. But he had no choice. This was one of the rare times Ramkrishna saw Baldev Das lose his composure. Tears welled up in the older man's eyes.

'What am I to do with him, Ramkrishna? Basant Las is older than you, yet he remains a child in temperament. Ramkrishna, always remember that words have the power to wound. So, be very mindful of what you say to people,' said Baldev Das, wiping his eyes with the edge of his dhoti.

Ramkrishna had always hoped his association with Baldev Das would last for a long time. However, their partnership came to an untimely end due to the older man's ill health.

The Calcutta share market was experiencing high volatility and the firm had incurred losses. Baldev Das, along with the partnership firm, had decided to slow down operations. To make matters worse, Baldev Das was bedridden due to his poor health.

Ramkrishna chafed at the inactivity. His restless mind did not allow him to remain idle for long—he needed to be in the thick of action at all times. As business was slow in Calcutta, he wanted to go to Bombay, where the action was.

He went to see Baldev Das.

'Bare Babuji, I am going to Bombay. There is nothing happening in Calcutta, and I am getting restless,' said Ramkrishna as he pulled up a chair and sat near Baldev Das's bed. The older man now spent most of his time in bed and only a very few people were allowed access to his room. Ramkrishna was deeply saddened to see his mentor lying in bed, immobilized.

'Ramkrishna, I know that if I tell you not to go, you will disobey me and go anyway. So, I won't say anything,' Baldev Das said with great effort. Even speaking exhausted him. He lifted his hand slightly and patted Ramkrishna's hand as if giving his permission.

Ramkrishna's maternal uncle, Motilal, had contacts in Bombay and helped his nephew set up shop there. Ramkrishna soon established himself in the cotton market and, in no time, became known as a big speculator in Bombay as well. The business was good, and he earned lakhs of rupees in profit within a short time.

One day, he received a telegram from his brother Jaidayal. It simply stated that Baldev Das's health had deteriorated further.

Ramkrishna rushed to Calcutta to see his mentor. He found him frail and in failing health. Baldev Das was all skin and bones and had tears in his eyes. It seemed he knew his days on earth were numbered.

Ramkrishna was torn between duty and gain. On one hand, his duty was to stay in Calcutta, spend time with and look after his mentor—a man who had taught him many life and business lessons and had taken him under his wing. On the other hand, there was the lure of monetary gain in Bombay. The speculation business was booming there, and Ramkrishna was making large profits. He had established himself in the trader community in Bombay and was enjoying the importance he was being given as a big speculator and wealthy man. He found Bombay to be far more exciting than Calcutta.

The dilemma was real. He knew he had to choose between the critical health of Baldev Das and the critical health of his business in Bombay.

Ramkrishna chose monetary gain and returned to Bombay. Baldev Das did not say a word or attempt to hold him back but had tears streaming down his cheeks as Ramkrishna said goodbye.

A few days after reaching Bombay, Ramkrishna received another telegram from Jaidayal informing him that Baldev Das was now very critical, and the doctors believed that the end was imminent.

A wave of guilt overtook Ramkrishna. He dropped everything and rushed to Calcutta. But he was too late. Baldev Das had passed away before he could reach him.

Ramkrishna was inconsolable. It felt as though a large hole had been ripped in his being. He remembered losing his father when he was barely out of his teens. This time, the loss was more palpable. Baldev Das had been his mentor, guide, sounding board, conscience keeper and more. To Ramkrishna, it was like losing another father; he could not imagine life without him. Nonetheless, he vowed to himself that he would strive to live the rest of his life guided by the ideals of Baldev Das.

8
Ramkrishna's Brother Jaidayal Grows Up

RAMKRISHNA and his family were doing well. Jaidayal was growing into a fine young man. Durga, despite her fragile health, continued to be the heart of the family. Jadiya Devi was Ramkrishna's conscience keeper. Yet, it was Rama, Ramkrishna and Durga's daughter, who was the apple of everyone's eye—especially her father's.

While Ramkrishna was building his wealth through the speculation market, his family quietly supported him, living their lives without fanfare. They had moved out of poverty and out of their one-room tenement, but their lifestyle remained simple. Never into outward displays of wealth, the family kept a low profile. However, the women in the household could now buy more jewellery, and without fear of Ramkrishna stealing it to pay off a debt!

Ramkrishna's brother Jaidayal had grown up during their time in Calcutta and eventually married. Soon after Rama was born, Jaidayal married Krishna. By then, the family had acquired wealth from the profits of Ramkrishna's successful silver trades, and there was no shortage of proposals for Jaidayal once he turned a teenager.

At the time of his marriage, Jaidayal was just fourteen, while Krishna was a young girl of twelve. She was wiry and fair, and Jaidayal was also very fair and good-looking. Though Krishna was not educated, Ramkrishna did not let that deter her marriage to his brother. He was certain that once she started living with the family, she would learn to read and write, just as his own wife, Durga, had improved her reading and writing skills after marriage. During the wedding, Ramkrishna took special care to ensure that Jaidayal was dressed in fine clothes and adorned with jewellery. His love for Jaidayal was similar to the parental love that Baldev Das had for Ramkrishna. Jaidayal, in turn, reciprocated this love throughout his life. In later years, people likened Ramkrishna and Jaidayal to the sun and the moon—different yet inseparable.

As was the practice in those days, Krishna returned to her parents' home after the wedding ceremony. By the time she came back to Ramkrishna's family, they had moved to a large house on Cornwallis Lane, and Ramkrishna had even bought a motorcar. He allowed Jaidayal to drive it, and Jaidayal would often ferry his wife and mother to the Ganga to bathe. Durga was unable to accompany them due to her fragile health.

Rama's birth had been nothing short of a miracle, as Durga had suffered several miscarriages before her. Following Rama's birth, Durga became pregnant again, but the child was delivered via a c-section and was stillborn. Durga remained unconscious for a long time after this ordeal, and her health declined. Motilal, Ramkrishna's uncle, got the best doctors in Calcutta to treat her, but she remained frail and her condition continued to deteriorate, with her temperature fluctuating between 106 and 96 degrees Fahrenheit.

Ramkrishna, Jaidayal, their mother and Krishna all took turns caring for Durga. As the elder daughter-in-law, Durga had a special place in the family. Ramkrishna even arranged for several brahmins and priests to pray for her recovery. Despite their efforts, Durga remained weak, unable to move or even raise her head to drink water.

Ramkrishna was almost frantic, haunted by memories of Narbada's illness and untimely death. He did not want Durga to die and felt wholly responsible for her wellbeing. When Durga stopped responding to active treatment, Ramkrishna remembered the words of Harjimal, his father, who had often said, 'The Ganga's waters are like medicine, and Narayana is the physician.'

He wanted to follow Harjimal's words and leave Durga's recovery in the hands of God. However, the family did not want to give up treatment entirely. Thus, except for a weekly injection administered by Dr Adalbehram, all other treatments were stopped. Durga was given small amounts of milk and mangoes, her favourite fruit. The family continued to pray for her health and made sure she sipped Ganga jal every day.

Whether it was the weekly injections or the power of their prayers and Ganga jal, Durga's health began to improve slowly but surely. Eventually, she was able to sit up and even talk. During this period, Ramkrishna promised his mother that he would not remarry if Durga did not recover. He also stopped going to the market and gave up speculation for a while.

However, when destiny is determined to smile on someone, every activity becomes beneficial. Ramkrishna had entered some trades in the silver market, but due to Durga's illness, he had been unable to settle them and close the positions. During those days, silver prices rose significantly, and Ramkrishna, due to those open positions, made several lakhs in profit. He took this as a blessing from God for looking after his wife.

Durga eventually made a recovery, but she was unable to have another child and remained in frail health for the rest of her life.

Jaidayal had been studying in Calcutta, but after his marriage, he dropped out of school. Around this time, Mahatma Gandhi had launched the Non-Cooperation Movement. A large rally was held in Calcutta Square, and Jaidayal, now out of school, attended it. The rally was massive, with many people present. Gandhi spoke in his trademark soft voice. Despite the lack of loudspeakers, he was heard by all as there was a pin-drop silence in the large gathering.

As was common during such rallies, the police arrived and arrested many attendees. Jaidayal, too, was taken into custody. However, his short stature came in handy as the police thought he was a minor and released him.

With no school to attend, Jaidayal had nothing to do. Ramkrishna wanted him to join the speculation and trading business, but Jaidayal's heart and interest were not in it. Ramkrishna was a man of action, unable to remain idle for long, with a mind that was perpetually active and engaged. Much as he loved his younger brother, he could not understand the young boy's inactivity.

Ramkrishna's Brother Jaidayal Grows Up

One morning, as Ramkrishna was leaving for work, he saw Jaidayal sitting in the front courtyard, staring into space. Ramkrishna felt a surge of irritation.

'Jaidayal, what are you doing? What is your plan for the day?' He fired off the questions as he walked purposefully towards the younger man.

'Oh, Bhaiji! You are going to work?' Jaidayal broke out of his reverie, looking up at his brother, who had by then reached his side.

'Yes, it is indeed me. What are planning to do today?' Ramkrishna asked, watching as Jaidayal struggled to sit up in his cane chair.

'Bhaiji, I have nothing planned. I will take the day as it comes,' Jaidayal replied, stretching his arms over his head and stifling a yawn.

'Jaidayal, you have to do something with your life. You must do something. You can't sit idle all day. You're married now. Come with me and learn the trade,' Ramkrishna said assertively.

'Bhaiji, I'm really not interested in speculation and trading,' Jaidayal said, his tone laced with complaint.

'But why? All our wealth comes from these activities. It is not a bad thing,' Ramkrishna countered, unable to understand how his brother could dismiss the very work that had lifted them out of poverty.

'But Bhaiji, you know that speculators are seen as gamblers in the market. They may have money, but they do not get the respect an industrialist gets—someone who owns factories. I like working with my hands. I also want respect. Why don't you consider starting a factory?' Jaidayal reasoned.

'Because my heart is not in it, Jaidayal! And remember, I am not a gambler. Yes, I speculate and trade, but it is based on my knowledge of the market and my instincts,' Ramkrishna was quick to explain.

Jaidayal nodded as if in agreement.

'So, we have a peculiar problem, Jaidayal. The work I do and know doesn't excite you. The work you want to do doesn't excite me. Chalo, let me see what I can do,' said Ramkrishna with a wry laugh.

Once he made up his mind, Ramkrishna acted swiftly. Armed with the knowledge that his brother enjoyed working with his hands, Ramkrishna looked for opportunities. He soon found one.

Near the French Motorcar Company on Circular Road in Calcutta was a motor workshop called Victor Company. Ramkrishna asked his brother if working in a motor workshop appealed to him, and Jaidayal agreed.

Ramkrishna purchased Victor Company, and Jaidayal started working there as well as managing it. He worked alongside the mechanics to learn how motorcars operated. Jaidayal may not have been interested in speculation or trading, but he was intelligent, sharp of mind and unafraid of hard work.

Jaidayal found working with his hands and the mechanics oddly satisfying. He would work all day without feeling tired. Before long, he could repair any motorcar that came to the workshop. He could overhaul engines and diagnose problems just by listening to the sound of the engine. As the overall supervisor, he gained confidence in his abilities and learnt to manage a team of people who were much older than him.

Unfortunately, Ramkrishna faced some adverse trades in the market and needed quick money. He decided to sell the motor workshop, and Jaidayal went back to being idle.

Ramkrishna's Brother Jaidayal Grows Up

It was then that Ramkrishna and his mother requested Motilal to employ Jaidayal. He agreed. Motilal was a silver dealer and sourced silver bricks from Bombay, which were then cut into smaller pieces for resale.

For any Marwari, it is essential to sit at the accounts table and learn the basics of accounting and cash flows before delving into anything else. Jaidayal was no exception and was asked to sit with the munim to understand the fundamentals of bookkeeping. Though he had managed the car workshop, Jaidayal found that the complexities of running a trading business were very different.

He learnt how cash was transferred between Calcutta and Bombay. Motilal sourced silver bricks from Bombay and, upon their receipt, had to send cash payments to the sellers. Bank transfers incurred significant fees, so an innovative system was used to minimize costs.

Motilal's accountant would withdraw notes in hundred-rupee denominations from the bank. The transaction didn't incur charges as it was from their own account. Once the munim had the notes, they were cut in half. One bundle of one half of the notes would be packed and sent to the seller through the post office. As a safety measure, the notes were insured for Rs 100. The second bundle of the other half of the notes would be packed and sent through the post office to the same seller. This time the insurance bought would be for Rs 300.

Once both bundles reached Bombay, the bundle with the lower insurance amount was delivered to the seller's address. The second bundle had to be collected by the seller from the post office. This method cost a fraction of what banks charged and did not take much time either.

Jaidayal discovered that there were almost no cases of cash bundles being lost. He asked the munim how they handled situations where a bundle did go missing.

'It is simple, Jaidayal. If one bundle gets lost, we can take the other bundle to the bank and deposit the notes there,' the munim explained. He liked the earnest young man's curious mind.

'So, does the bank hand over the full amount there and then?' Jaidayal asked incredulously. His sharp mind was already thinking of ways the banks could be scammed.

'No, no, of course not. Banks don't hand over the entire amount immediately. They are not fools,' the munim replied quickly.

'Then how do they handle it?' Jaidayal leaned forward, impatiently awaiting the munim's explanation.

'The banks follow a system,' the munim began. A staff member approached with a ledger for review, but he waved him away, keen to explain the process to Jaidayal.

'When we submit the notes, the banks check if notes with the same serial numbers have been deposited with any other bank. They ask us to wait for a certain period while they verify. Once they confirm that the other bundle has not been submitted at any bank, they give us the full amount,' the munim explained proudly, as though the system were his own invention.

'Ah! What a novel way of transferring money,' Jaidayal remarked, impressed. Then another thought struck him.

'But how do they prevent double payment? Someone could take the other bundle to the bank after the verification period, submit it and get the money. Couldn't that happen?' Jaidayal thought he had found the flaw in the system.

The munim, it seemed, was ready for this question. 'Each note has a serial number, does it not?' he asked. Jaidayal nodded.

'So, when the bank pays us the full amount, they cancel the serial numbers of the submitted notes. This information is sent to every bank. Thus, if anyone tries to act smart, they will be caught. Not only that, but they will also be handed over to the police for attempted fraud,' the munim explained triumphantly, as if daring Jaidayal to find another flaw in the system. He was confident there were none, as many traders used this method.

Jaidayal found his experiences at the motorcar workshop and his uncle's office invaluable. He would use many of the lessons he had learnt during this time when Ramkrishna eventually became an industrialist.

9

The Apple of Ramkrishna's Eye—His Daughter Rama

RAMA was growing up and remained the apple of Ramkrishna's eye. There had been four pregnancies after Rama but the children, all boys, were either stillborn or died immediately after birth. After the fourth failed pregnancy Durga's health had failed. Ramkrishna did not have any other child with Durga.

Rama, for the first seven years of her life, was the only child in the family. In 1924, Jaidayal and Krishna had their first child—a son they named Vishnu Hari. Ramkrishna believed that Rama had brought good fortune to the family. Thus, he took special care to ensure that the young girl had access to reading and writing from an early age. He wanted her to receive the best education possible, something he could now easily afford as a wealthy man.

By the time Rama was five years old, she could read Sanskrit books. While she could read the words, some of which were complex, as a small child, she was unable to grasp their full meaning. Her spiritual learning came from her grandmother, her mother, and later her aunt Krishna. When she was eight, Ramkrishna sent her to the Bhagwat Bhakti Ashram to further her education.

Rama, a serious child, had a quiet demeanour and an inclination towards spirituality. She would ask questions about the soul and *atma* and listened intently to the explanations given. When she was nine, she accompanied her parents to Haridwar. While walking along the riverbank, a sharp thorn pricked her foot.

As her foot began to bleed, Ramkrishna, concerned, immediately bent down to check if she was in pain. He was surprised by his daughter's calm response.

'Bapuji, the pain is only to my body. I am *atma*, which cannot feel any pain,' Rama told him.

Ramkrishna, himself a deeply spiritual man, looked at her with both amazement and pride. His pride grew manyfold a year later. In the mid-1920s, a large Marwari Sabha was held in Bombay. This was a regular event where the Marwari community gathered to discuss and deliberate on a variety of subjects. This particular event had several thousand attendees. In front of this large crowd, the young Rama delivered an extempore speech in Hindi on the importance of spirituality. The entire gathering rose to their feet to applaud her as she finished speaking. The president of the Marwari Sabha, Ranglal Jajodia, was so moved that he announced the award of a gold medal to honour her.

Ramkrishna, not having had a formal education himself, left no stone unturned to educate Rama and provide her with a well-rounded learning experience. As a result, Rama became proficient in English, Hindi and Sanskrit. She was a good swimmer, learnt horse riding and knew how to ride a bicycle as well as drive a car.

By the time Rama turned fifteen, she was considered well into marriageable age by the standards of the time. Aware of this, Ramkrishna had been looking for a suitable boy for her. He wanted the best match for Rama. She was dark-skinned and tall for her age, but she was also well-read. Ramkrishna wanted someone who could match her mental stature.

He looked everywhere and asked everyone he knew for recommendations, but he did not think of asking Rama. He knew that she was so obedient that even if he were to choose a dark, ugly or short man as her groom, she would agree without a murmur.

Shanti Prasad Jain was a young man in his early twenties. Six years older than Rama, he was from Najibabad, a town in Uttar Pradesh, and belonged to a family of landlords and financiers. They were known as the Sahu Jain family—Sahu being the equivalent of Seth or a moneylender.

Shanti Prasad had lost his father at a young age and realized early on that he had to make a life for himself and could not depend on the family. He was an intelligent man with a head for finance, commerce and economics. He had earned his bachelor's degree from Meerut College, a premier institution of the time. Adding to his appeal, Shanti Prasad was fair and good-looking.

Ramkrishna, unable to find a groom he liked, placed a matrimonial advertisement. The Sahu Jain family saw the

The Apple of Ramkrishna's Eye—His Daughter Rama

advertisement and responded on behalf of Shanti Prasad. The advertisement had generated hundreds of responses, and the Dalmia family meticulously went through each of them. Ramkrishna was looking for an educated Bania boy from a good family. He was particularly impressed by Shanti Prasad's education and background.

The Jain family, on its part, liked Rama for her simplicity, Gandhian upbringing and her love for culture and literature. Both families approved of the match, and the marriage was finalized. The Dalmia family was delighted, as this was to be the first wedding of the next generation. Jaidayal and Krishna's children were still toddlers.

However, a message from Jagmandar Das, an elder relative of Shanti Prasad, worried the Dalmia family. Jagmandar Das informed them that the *baraat* would include a large number of people and that the Jain family expected everyone to be treated very well. This, the Dalmia family understood, meant that a lot of money had to be spent for the wedding.

At the time, Ramkrishna was going through one of his lean phases and had no liquid cash available for the lavish wedding ceremonies and hosting the baraat. When Motilal learnt of this, he offered to host the entire wedding in his home and bear all the expenses.

However, Jadiya Devi, Ramkrishna's mother, wouldn't hear of it. This was to be the wedding of the first child of the next generation. Moreover, Ramkrishna was regarded as a wealthy man. She knew that allowing her brother to host the wedding would harm Ramkrishna's reputation and the name of the Dalmia family.

She thanked her brother and explained the matter to him. Motilal, being a worldly-wise man himself, understood and wished his sister well.

Jadiya Devi went to Chirawa to the old family home, where Durga's jewellery was stored. The ornaments, nearly new because Durga, due to her fragile health, had few occasions to wear them, were brought back to Calcutta.

Motilal offered to keep the ornaments in his custody and extend a loan against them.

'Why sell the family jewellery, sister? I know you do not want to take money from me. Think of it as a loan against these fine ornaments,' Motilal reasoned.

Once again, Jadiya Devi refused her brother's offer.

'When Ramkrishna earns back the money, he can reclaim his wife's ornaments,' Motilal tried one final time.

However, Jadiya Devi did not want to be under any obligation, especially for this wedding. She discussed the matter with Ramkrishna, who agreed with her. They took the ornaments to a jeweller and sold them, raising enough money to host a wedding that met the expected high standards.

Rama and Shanti Prasad were married in 1932. Thus, Ramkrishna gained a son who was to go on to become a trusted business partner as well.

10
Baby Steps—From Speculator to Industrialist

RAMA was Ramkrishna's only child, and he thought the world of her. He could not bear for her to be away from him. He proposed, therefore, that Shanti Prasad move in with the Dalmia family.

Shanti Prasad had lost his father at a young age. His brother, Shriyans Prasad Jain, had been adopted by Ganesh Lal, a wealthy merchant, leaving Shanti Prasad to fend for himself. Thus, he had no hesitation in accepting Ramkrishna's offer.

There was a seven-year age difference between Shanti Prasad and Jaidayal. Both men were intelligent and had a head for business. Both looked up to Ramkrishna—one as an elder brother and the other as a surrogate father. Neither had any interest in speculation or in the share market, which was

Ramkrishna's domain. Further, as young men in their twenties, they were eager to do more than just trade in the share market or speculate in commodities. They also realized that money alone did not generate respect in the community; true respect came from earning money through industry.

One evening as the three men were having dinner at home, Jaidayal broached the topic of setting up something other than share trading. The family was now living in Bihta, a village in south Bihar, and Ramkrishna would travel to Calcutta or Bombay whenever his satta bazaar business required it.

'Bhaiji, you know I was very happy when I was running the motor workshop,' said Jaidayal, tearing off a piece of chapatti.

'You mean you liked getting your hands dirty with oil and God knows what?' Ramkrishna teased lightly, taking a bite of chapatti dipped in dal.

'Bhaiji, you are making fun of me. But I want to do something to earn big money,' said Jaidayal as he focused on the chapatti and sabzi on his plate.

'There's big money to be made in the satta bazaar, you know,' countered Ramkrishna with a gleam in his eye. He glanced at Shanti Prasad to gauge his reaction. Shanti Prasad, however, kept his eyes on his plate.

'But there is no respect in it, Bhaiji. Surely you know this. Look at you—you are richer than most industrialists in Calcutta. But do people treat you the same way they treat others, like the Birla brothers or even the Bajorias?' Jaidayal said, his tone laced with frustration. It pained him to see his brother denied the respect given to industrialists.

Ramkrishna listened silently. He recalled a conversation with Jaidayal from the time he had bought the car workshop for him. Jaidayal had told him that while speculation in the satta

Baby Steps—From Speculator to Industrialist

bazaar might bring wealth for the Dalmias, it didn't earn the respect that came with being an industrialist. The thought had been rankling him, but Ramkrishna had not allowed himself to reflect on it. Caught up in the routine of life and the thrill of speculating, he hadn't seriously considered doing any other business.

Ramkrishna was an avid risk-taker and needed the excitement of trading. However, he was also an intelligent man who understood that to gain true respect within the industry and to be able to sit at the high table, he needed to be more than just a satte-baaz. He knew he had the money to set up any factory he desired, but he also knew he couldn't run it on his own.

Now, as Jaidayal brought up the subject again, an idea began forming in Ramkrishna's mind. He turned to his son-in-law.

'Shanti Prasad, what do you think? Do you agree with Jaidayal?' asked Ramkrishna. He had noticed Shanti Prasad keeping his eyes downcast during the conversation between Jaidayal and himself and wanted to hear his thoughts.

Shanti Prasad, being directly addressed, was forced to look up from his plate. Before answering Ramkrishna, he glanced at Jaidayal as if seeking his permission to speak. Ramkrishna, catching this exchange, realized that the two younger men had already discussed this matter.

'So, Shanti Prasad, there is no respect in satte-bazzi, eh?' Ramkrishna prodded his son-in-law.

'Pitaji, as you know, my father died when I was very young, and I never had a business to run. I have had to make my own way in life. But I have observed people closely. What Chacha ji is saying resonates with me too. Speculation can make you very wealthy, but industry—even a small factory—will earn you disproportionate respect,' said Shanti Prasad, his tone calm yet strong.

Ramkrishna looked keenly from one man to the other, his mind ticking. He gazed at the ceiling in deep thought. The two younger men had forgotten about the food on their plates and were looking at him without blinking.

As Ramkrishna stared upward, he closed his eyes briefly, nodded to himself as if reaching a decision, and then looked at the two men who were waiting expectantly.

'So, if I set up a factory, will you both run it? You know my heart lies in the market. Will you be able to take on the responsibility?' Ramkrishna asked.

The younger men looked at each other and then turned to Ramkrishna. From their expressions, he could tell that they did not entirely believe him. So, he repeated the question.

'Of course, yes, of course! We will take the responsibility,' they replied almost in unison, smiling widely.

'Bhaiji, you know how well I ran the workshop. I also quickly learnt about machines, engines and all their various parts. I know I can pick up anything to do with machinery just as fast. And Shanti Prasad here has a head for business—you know that already, don't you? So, which factory are you thinking of setting up?' Jaidayal asked eagerly, his words tumbling out in a rush.

'Hold on, hold on, young man. Not so fast. Now that we have had this talk, let us wait some time before deciding what to do and where,' Ramkrishna said, patting his brother on the head. He also glanced at Shanti Prasad and nodded to him.

Jaidayal and Shanti Prasad nodded back happily.

The opportunity to set up a factory presented itself not long after that conversation.

In late 1932, the British government increased the import duty on sugar to promote domestic manufacturing. Sugar was always in high demand and there was great interest among businessmen to set up sugar factories. Ramkrishna believed he had found the perfect product to launch his industrial journey.

Though he was a wealthy man, the bulk of his wealth was tied up in the share and commodity markets. Even when he earned money, he would donate generously to the needy and poor and contribute regularly to the Indian National Congress (INC). Thus, he lacked the ready cash needed to start a manufacturing business.

Ramkrishna had a habit of keeping large sums of money in his pocket. His mother, who had seen enough cycles of fasting and feasting, knew that Ramkrishna would earn money but also lose it in the market. So, the wily older woman had instructed Durga to take money from Ramkrishna's pocket whenever possible and deposit it with Motilal for safekeeping. This had been going on for quite a few years, and while the women believed Ramkrishna was unaware of it, he, sharp man that he was, knew. However, he did not mind, rationalizing that the money was being saved rather than spent on ornaments, and could be utilized whenever needed.

When Ramkrishna decided to venture into the sugar manufacturing business, he turned to this pool of savings. Jadiya Devi and Durga were happy that the money would be used for productive purposes rather than being reinvested in the satta bazaar.

Although Ramkrishna had a high-risk appetite in the satta market, this was his first foray into industry. He decided to proceed with caution and spread his risk.

He had been eyeing an established sugar mill in Bihta for quite some time. It had been set up by a rich villager named Nirmal Kumar. Though the mill was rudimentary, Ramkrishna saw it as a good starting point.

Ramkrishna and Jaidayal went to Bihta to meet Nirmal Kumar and proposed a partnership. The idea was for the Dalmias and Nirmal Kumar to run the mill together. Although Nirmal Kumar had set up the mill, he was finding it difficult to manage it. Even though he was rich, operating the mill was expensive, and it required a good administrator, which he was not. He jumped at the offer.

Ramkrishna and Jaidayal inspected the small mill and the surrounding area. Ramkrishna appreciated that some groundwork had already been done. However, he realized that expanding the mill would require more land and machinery. He had thoughts around both.

Nirmal Kumar was a well-known zamindar in the area. He knew the villagers who owned the land around the mill. He told Ramkrishna that he would help in acquiring the land, but it would take time. Each landowner would need to be spoken with and convinced to sell their land.

'How much time do you think it will take to buy the land we need, Nirmal bhai?' Ramkrishna asked.

'We will need to talk to at least a hundred or so landowners as the land holdings are small. So, I think I can say that it will take a year or so,' replied Nirmal Kumar without showing any urgency.

'A year?' Ramkrishna spluttered. He was used to dealing in markets that moved within minutes, where even a day was too long. And here his business partner was talking about a whole year.

'A year is too long. After that, we will still need time to expand the factory and import machinery. The entire situation could change in a year,' Ramkrishna said briskly.

'But that is the way it is, Sethji,' argued Nirmal Kumar languidly. Now that he had a wealthy business partner, he assumed good times lay ahead.

'How much does the land cost?' asked Ramkrishna sharply.

'About Rs 10 per bigha,' replied Nirmal Kumar.

Ramkrishna thought for a moment. He closed his eyes and made some mental calculations. When he opened them, his mind was made up.

'Tell the villagers we will pay Rs 100 per bigha, but only if they sell within the next two weeks. Those who want to sell at this rate can come to us and do the paperwork. Also, tell them that if we do not get enough land, we will take our mill elsewhere,' he instructed Nirmal Kumar.

Nirmal Kumar was stunned. He thought Ramkrishna had heard the cost of land incorrectly.

'Sethji, I said the cost is Rs 10 per bigha, not Rs 100,' Nirmal Kumar said slowly, as though correcting a child.

'I know, Nirmal bhai. Now do as I have told you to,' Ramkrishna replied curtly. He did not like the other man's tone.

As he saw his business partner deflate in front of his eyes, he realized he needed to soften his approach.

'Don't worry, Nirmal bhai. I have a plan for this sugar mill. Money will not be a problem. Please announce the offer to the villagers,' he reassured him.

The offer was made public, and the villagers, seeing it as a windfall, eagerly accepted.

Meanwhile, Ramkrishna explained the plan for the mill to Nirmal Kumar. He proposed converting the mill company into a joint stock company, with Nirmal Kumar and the Dalmias serving as the managing agency.

The managing agency system had, in fact, evolved during the second quarter of the nineteenth century in India. It was adopted by London as an efficient way to manage joint stock companies operating in the Indian subcontinent, especially when the shareholders of such companies had no first-hand knowledge of the business. The system worked as follows: the managing agency essentially operated as an entrepreneur. When it identified a business opportunity—for example, a cotton mill—it raised venture capital from friends and associates of the managing agent or promoter. Any funding shortfall was borrowed from a bank.

With the funds in hand, the managing agency bought the mill and set it up to operate. Once the mill and the business were running successfully, the managing agency sold its majority shareholding to the public, turning the company into a listed entity. However, the managing agency signed a long-term management contract with the company, which gave it the right to continue to manage the business. The profits earned by the managing agency became capital that could be invested in other businesses, such as a flour mill. Despite its small shareholding, the managing agency maintained control of the cotton mill due to its long-term management contract.

Typically, the managing agency made key decisions on behalf of its operating companies, such as determining which products to manufacture, which markets to target and where to source the raw materials. The advantage of the managing agency system was that it enabled the agency to control and run several enterprises with a small financial stake in each. Its

Baby Steps—From Speculator to Industrialist

ability to raise capital from banks and the public depended on the promoter's track record and reputation.

Nirmal Kumar was excited about the idea and readily agreed. Ramkrishna told him that he would sell the shares though his networks in Calcutta and Bombay.

A limited joint stock company was formed, and Ramkrishna successfully sold the shares, raising the necessary funds to purchase the land and machinery.

Ramkrishna made Jaidayal responsible for overseeing the mill's expansion and operations. The younger man embraced the exercise with enthusiasm, delighted to finally be doing something useful.

The machinery was ordered, and work on the expansion of the factory began. Jaidayal spent his days at the site, sometimes staying till midnight to supervise the progress. Within a year, the expanded mill was ready to start production.

It was now that Jaidayal's experience in running the motor workshop proved invaluable. As with any new set-up, the sugar mill faced teething problems with its machinery. However, Jaidayal was able to understand and solve the problems easily. Some of the older workers and machine operators viewed him as a novice as he had never worked in a factory before, and would sometimes challenge him. However, the young man remained true to his convictions.

On one occasion, when the workers were unable to resolve an issue with a machine, Jaidayal came to take a look at it.

'What is the problem here, bhaiyon?' he asked, peering into the innards of the large machine.

'Sethji, this machine has stopped working on its own,' a worker replied matter-of-factly.

'No machine stops working on its own, bhai,' said Jaidayal, rolling up the sleeves of his kurta as he prepared to investigate.

'Have you checked this part?' he asked, pointing to a small part after a brief inspection.

'No, Sethji, we have not,' said the worker confidently.

'Then why don't you check it and restart the machine?' suggested Jaidayal, looking up at the worker from his half-bent position.

'But Sethji, this part is not the problem,' objected the worker, and the other workers nodded in agreement.

Jaidayal straightened up and looked at the gathered workers. He knew this was a test, as they believed he didn't know anything about machinery.

'Do as I say and see for yourself,' Jaidayal said firmly.

The workers exchanged glances, some suppressing smiles. They knew that unlike them, their Sethji had never worked in a sugar mill before. They were not going to take instructions from a novice.

'Sethji, we do not know how to remove and replace that part. We will need an expert mechanic, and it will cost the mill to hire him,' one worker offered as an excuse.

'Listen, bhai, get the expert mechanic and let him have a look. The mill will not have to pay him—I will pay him personally,' said Jaidayal, exasperated. He knew exactly what was going on.

The workers now had no choice but to obey. They looked at each other and nodded.

'And do it quickly. This is an important machine and it should not remain idle for long as it will affect production,' instructed Jaidayal as he walked away.

The expert mechanic was called in. He checked the part Jaidayal had pointed out and found that it was indeed the

Baby Steps—From Speculator to Industrialist

problem. He repaired and replaced it before instructing the foreman to start the machine.

All the workers gathered around, watching with bated breath to see if the machine would start. The foreman pulled the lever.

There was a brief moment of silence, and the workers felt vindicated. Then, with a loud click, the machine started humming. It was the sweetest sound to Jaidayal's ears.

A couple of workers sent up a small cheer, then glanced at the others for approval. A murmur went round and then grew into a full-fledged cheer.

'Sethji was right. We should not have doubted him,' was the general refrain among the workers.

Jaidayal gained instant credibility and went from strength to strength from then on.

The mill at Bihta was successful as sugar remained in high demand, and Ramkrishna was pleased that the mill was generating profits.

Within a short period of time, Ramkrishna gained two valuable insights from his experience with the sugar mill. The first was that the mill's revenue was not subject to great volatility. The mill produced sugar, the sugar was sold and after deducting expenses, a profit was generated. While the profit might fluctuate slightly, there was still a profit every month. This was vastly different from the satta market, which could see gains in one week and then absolute losses for months. Ramkrishna liked the fact that the mill generated a stable stream of income.

The second insight was surprising, even to him. He noticed a change in how people interacted with him. There was a different kind of respect when they dealt with him now. At first, he could not pinpoint the reason for this shift. Then it hit him. He remembered the conversation he had with Jaidayal, who had said that people generally respected businessmen who produced something tangible. Ramkrishna realized that all his conversations with people now began with them asking about the sugar mill.

Ramkrishna enjoyed the newfound respect he saw in other people's eyes. The sharp man that he was, he knew that the next phase of his life would revolve around businesses and industries. He reasoned that if a single sugar mill, where he was only a part owner with a non-family member, could bring about such a change in people's behaviour, then building an industrial group with many enterprises would catapult him to the top of the league.

Ramkrishna also gained another insight, which came from understanding himself. He knew he had the ability and mindset to take risks, but he also recognized that he could not run businesses on his own. He needed capable people to manage them. Instead of bringing in external partners, Ramkrishna decided that all future partnerships would involve Jaidayal and Shanti Prasad. He treated Shanti Prasad like the son he never had.

Jaidayal had already proven himself at the Bihta sugar mill, and Ramkrishna now wanted to induct Shanti Prasad into the business as well.

As the demand for sugar was still growing, Ramkrishna decided to set up another sugar mill, but this time, on his own. Still looking for a place in Bihar, he zeroed in on Dehri-on-Sone in the Rohtas district. Dehri, situated on the banks of the river Sone, was ideal. This town would later come to be known as Dalmianagar.

When Ramkrishna and Jaidayal inspected the site, they decided to build the mill near the railway station. Shanti Prasad was also included in the project. The land in the area was owned by farmers, and once again, Ramkrishna offered a price above the market rate to expedite the acquisition process. Simultaneously, orders for machinery were placed.

This was during the Civil Disobedience Movement launched by Gandhi, and the Swadeshi Movement had also regained momentum.

Ramkrishna, unlike some other wealthy people and industrialists, was not shy about supporting the INC with funds. He was a generous contributor to the cause and had direct contact with leaders like Gandhi, Sardar Patel, Rajendra Prasad and Muhammed Ali Jinnah. These leaders appreciated meeting and interacting with like-minded people, especially those who contributed financially to their parties.

Ramkrishna enjoyed hobnobbing with political leaders, recalling a statement made by his mentor Baldev Das. The older man had told him that associating with powerful, respected and well-known people would reflect positively on him. The world respected people of a certain kind, and being seen as one of them would enhance his own standing.

Whether or not these political leaders liked Ramkrishna personally is anybody's guess, but what they did appreciate was the generous financial contributions he made to themselves and their party. It was a symbiotic relationship—both sides benefited from it.

Ramkrishna knew that swadeshi was the buzzword at the time. Thus, when it came to ordering machines for the Dehri mill, he wanted to source them from local companies instead of importing them from the West. Ramkrishna had a friend, an Englishman, who managed the Calcutta-based Burn & Company. He placed the orders for the machines with this company. However, the company could not manufacture sugarcane-crushing machines, which had to be ordered from Glasgow.

As the sugar mill at Dehri was under construction, Ramkrishna had a thought.

'Jaidayal, sugarcane is not available throughout the year, is it?' he asked his younger brother.

'No, Bhaiji, sugarcane is usually harvested between December and March,' replied Jaidayal.

'Then does that mean the machines will be idle when there is no sugarcane?' asked Ramkrishna, looking keenly at Jaidayal.

'Bhaiji, as sugar is made from sugarcane juice, we need sugarcane to produce sugar. If there is no sugarcane, how can the machines produce anything at all?' responded Jaidayal.

'Can we store the sugarcane juice and use it to make sugar during the lean months?' Ramkrishna asked, his mind ticking. He did not like the idea of the machines lying idle for part of the year.

'I don't think so, Bhaiji. The juice will go rancid if we store it for too long,' explained Jaidayal, unsure where this line of questioning was headed.

'Hmm, that is a problem. It means we will incur the cost of the workers, but they will have no work, and it won't be their fault since we won't have the sugarcane to give them. It's too bad we cannot store the juice,' mused Ramkrishna aloud.

Then Ramkrishna stopped abruptly.

'What if we make gur and store that? Can sugar be made from gur?' he asked Jaidayal excitedly.

Baby Steps—From Speculator to Industrialist

'Yes, of course, Bhaiji. We can make gur, which can later be converted into sugar,' said Jaidayal slowly as he considered the possibilities. He now realized where his brother was going with this.

'Then we should make gur from the excess juice and store it. And even if we have to buy gur, we can during the lean months. That way, the mill will operate year-round,' said Ramkrishna decisively. The problem, in his mind, was solved.

It was a good suggestion, but producing sugar from gur required different machines than the ones installed in the factory. It was Burn & Company that offered to manufacture these machines.

The Dehri sugar mill was ready within a year. Ramkrishna entrusted Jaidayal with the full responsibility of running and managing it. He named the company Rohtas Sugar Ltd, which was also structured as a joint stock company with a managing agency system. The company's shares were easily sold in Calcutta and Bombay. Both Jaidayal and Shanti Prasad were made partners in the company as well as in the managing agency.

By now, Ramkrishna had full confidence in his 'right hand and left hand'—as he referred to Jaidayal and Shanti Prasad. The two younger men enjoyed running and managing the business as they had an aptitude for it. This left Ramkrishna free to explore other opportunities, raise funds for future expansions and pursue his political interests.

Ramkrishna had been a follower of the INC since 1918, a time when he had come into wealth after his successful silver deals on the London Exchange. His relationship with the INC was a symbiotic one. Political parties were happy to interact with wealthy individuals as they were constantly in need of financial support. Wealthy patrons, in turn, had their own mix of altruistic and self-serving reasons for maintaining close ties with political leaders.

As a devoted supporter of the INC, Ramkrishna was keen to do his bit for the freedom struggle. In 1920, as part of his commitment to the swadeshi movement, he made his entire family burn all foreign mill-made clothes and switch to wearing khadi. During a visit to Bombay, he removed the foreign caps people he met were wearing and threw them into a fire, allowing only those in Gandhi caps to keep them. Ramkrishna also appealed to everyone he met, in whichever city he visited, to wear only khadi.

Between that time and now, when he was the owner of two sugar mills, Ramkrishna had also established connections with many political leaders. He provided financial support to them and their families, sending monthly contributions ranging from Rs 250 to Rs 500. During the 1920s and 1930s, when many political leaders were jailed by the British government, often for long periods, Ramkrishna's contributions provided much-needed support to their families.

While many wealthy individuals and businessmen hesitated to openly support political leaders for fear of repercussions from the British government, Ramkrishna was fearless to the point of being foolhardy. Without worrying about the consequences, he actively supported the INC.

In 1934, elections were held for the Legislative Assembly, a form of general elections organized by the British in India. One seat was allocated for Delhi in the Assembly. Ramkrishna decided to contest the election from Delhi as the Congress candidate. However, Dr Rajendra Prasad, a Congress leader, nominated a close of friend of his for the seat. Ramkrishna felt hurt and upset. He had financially supported the Congress, as well as many of its leaders individually, for several years. Even Rajendra Prasad had been helped by him—Ramkrishna had made him a partner in the managing agency of his Bihta sugar mill.

Ramkrishna raised a minor fuss over the nomination for the Delhi seat, enough for Gandhi to send him a telegram requesting him to withdraw his nomination. Jamnalal Bajaj, an industrialist from Bombay and a Congress sympathizer, also sent Ramkrishna a telegram requesting him to withdraw his candidature. However, Ramkrishna was not easily swayed. He had his convictions.

He wired back to Gandhi, who was at Wardha at the time, suggesting that Gandhi arbitrate between Rajendra Prasad and himself to choose the best candidate for the seat. Ramkrishna assured Gandhi that if he did not believe Ramkrishna was the best man, then he would withdraw his candidature. He received no reply from Gandhi.

Since the Congress already had a candidate, Ramkrishna decided to stand as an independent. His family was dead against him fighting the election.

'You are a businessman, Bhaiji. Why do you want to be a politician?' asked Jaidayal, apprehensive about businessmen entering politics.

'Pitaji, you are friends with political leaders from all parties. If you are elected as a candidate, your relationships with all of them will no doubt suffer. Maybe our business will too,' Shanti Prasad voiced his own fears.

Besides his own family, Ramkrishna's decision created ripples within the Congress. Madan Mohan Malviya called him from Banaras, urging him not to stand as an independent but as a Hindu Mahasabha candidate. Ramkrishna politely declined. The finance minister of Bihar also approached him and asked him to fight the elections as their nominee. Ramkrishna agreed, but only if it aligned with Congress policy. While others hemmed and hawed, Ramkrishna stood firm on his decision to contest as an independent. He told Ganesh Dutt, a minister in the Bihar government, that his victory would be seen as a defeat of the Congress.

However, Ramkrishna did not win the election. He attributed his loss to false rumours suggesting he was a Muslim. His surname, 'Dalmia', ended in 'Mia'—a suffix often associated with Muslim names—and his opponents misled voters by focusing on this. They also claimed that, if elected, Ramkrishna would push for reducing sugarcane prices—a claim that resonated as everyone knew he owned sugar mills.

This was the first political election Ramkrishna had contested. Once it was over, he told his family that he was a novice and did not know the rules of the game. There were sixty polling booths in Delhi, but Ramkrishna did not visit a single one. Nor did he ask Jaidayal or Shanti Prasad to canvass at the booths. Only a few representatives, nominated by Ramkrishna, visited the polling stations.

Ramkrishna's decision to contest the election created a rift between him and other Congress leaders. Later, Jamnalal Bajaj took it upon himself to patch up the differences between Ramkrishna, Sardar Patel, Rajendra Prasad and other party leaders.

After his brief flirtation with electoral politics, Ramkrishna realized that the satta bazaar was better suited to him. He left the management of the sugar mills to the younger men in the family. The mills were doing well, and Ramkrishna raised more

Baby Steps—From Speculator to Industrialist

funds by selling more shares of Rohtas Sugar Ltd. Within a short time, the mill's production capacity increased by two and a half times.

Ramkrishna also acquired a majority stake in Light Railway, a company operating passenger and goods trains. He saw synergies between the two businesses, as sugar—his primary product—had to be transported to other parts of the country to be sold. Rail transport was both cheaper and faster than any other mode. In addition, he constructed a ropeway to bring sugarcane more quickly and efficiently to the factory in Dehri.

Confident that there was a steady revenue stream from his factories, Ramkrishna became even more active in the satta bazaar. The newfound financial security allowed him to take bigger risks, and he became a market maker. Traders would closely observe his deals. Depending on which way he was leaning, the market leaned accordingly. It was said that Ramkrishna could make the market 'dance to his tune'. He dealt in the forward markets for jute, cotton and silver—large commodities with forward deliveries. Ramkrishna found himself enjoying the satta market even more now that he had other businesses going.

Between 1933 and 1936, Ramkrishna set up several more factories in Dehri, including a paper factory. He had noticed that the byproduct of sugar manufacturing, bagasse—the fibre left after crushing sugarcane—was being burned in boilers to generate steam for running the crushing and other machines.

Ramkrishna observed that paper was made using bamboo and other types of grasses. He reasoned that bagasse could be used as a substitute for these materials. He launched a pilot project with his factory workers. It worked. Ramkrishna instructed Jaidayal and Shanti Prasad to set up a paper factory.

They imported a special machine capable of manufacturing various types of paper. The factory produced white paper for writing, craft paper for packaging, and duplex and triplex papers for specialized purposes.

Jaidayal and Shanti Prasad focused on the factory, production and sales, while Ramkrishna concentrated on generating new ideas and securing financing. This team worked well and was instrumental in transforming the small industry in Dehri to one of India's largest industrial empires.

The team became known as the Dalmia-Jain Group, and Dehri came to be called Dalmianagar.

11

Ramkrishna Takes on the Mighty ACC

BY the end of 1933, Ramkrishna was on a roll. He had several factories running and an investment company in Calcutta. Named Dalmia Investment Company Limited, it transacted business in primary and secondary securities. He was now recognized as an industrialist rather than merely a speculator.

Ramkrishna divided his time between Dalmianagar and trips to Calcutta and Bombay, leaving his brother and son-in-law to manage the factories in Dalmianagar. To improve communications, he installed a private trunk telephone line between Dalmianagar and Calcutta. A trunk line used one central line that branched into multiple connections for handling inbound and outbound calls. Its private nature ensured that only people in Dalmianagar and Ramkrishna's office in Calcutta could access it. Ramkrishna was among the first industrialists in India to have his own private trunk telephone line.

He was also among the first, if not the first, industrialists to own a private plane. It was a three-seater aircraft that he used to travel between cities. On one occasion, while in Gaya for work, he needed to go to Calcutta. One of his associates, Haridas Gayadeen, was with him. Both men took the plane. However, shortly after takeoff, Haridas experienced heart palpitations, and the plane had to turn back. As Ramkrishna needed to go to Calcutta urgently, he took the night train instead.

The next morning, two of Ramkrishna's distant relatives who worked with him decided to take the plane to Calcutta. During takeoff, the plane collided with some oil drums and burst into flames. Fortunately, the crew and passengers were rescued with only minor injuries. When Ramkrishna learnt about the accident, he counted his blessings and thanked God. Throughout his life, he remained religiously inclined and followed the Hindu dharma.

As a devout Hindu, Ramkrishna did feel the need to have a son. By then, his brother had three sons. Though Ramkrishna looked upon Jaidayal and Shanti Prasad as sons, he still harboured a deep desire to have a son of his own. He knew that Durga could not have any more children. Thus, if he wanted a son, he would have to marry again. Legally, a man could marry multiple times then, as the Hindu Marriage Act came into effect only in 1955. While he did think of remarriage, his busy work life prevented him from taking any steps. Trading and speculation were going well, and the factories were running smoothly. He put aside the thought of a son and concentrated on building an industrial empire. He had come to appreciate the power associated with industry and wanted to grow even bigger.

Ramkrishna had a keen ability to analyse risk and conduct cost-benefit analyses quickly. After setting up factories, he realized there were other ways to expand his empire. He recognized that his financial heft and large network in the stock market gave him the ability to buy companies and use the managing agency system to run them. Even a small shareholding would enable Ramkrishna to control a company.

One of the first businesses he acquired was Bharat Insurance Ltd. Established in 1896, the company's business had seen little growth. By 1935–36, Ramkrishna had his eye on this company. He understood the business and believed it would complement his existing companies.

Ramkrishna's approach to buying something he wanted was to offer a price higher than the market rate. He followed this strategy with Bharat Insurance as well, offering to pay double the market price to buy the controlling shareholding. Luckily for him, the company was not doing well financially, and people were wary of insuring their lives through it.

After acquiring the controlling share, Ramkrishna appointed Jaidayal as the administrator while maintaining oversight of the company himself. He nurtured it back to health, and by the time of Indian independence, Bharat Insurance was ranked among the top five insurance companies in India. It had a high business volume, a low expense ratio, good interest yields and was a stable and sound business.

Later, when the insurance industry was nationalized through an Ordinance issued on 19 January 1956, Bharat Insurance, along with all other insurance companies in India, was acquired by the government and amalgamated into the Life Insurance Corporation (LIC). LIC absorbed 154 Indian and 16 non-Indian insurers, as well as 75 provident societies—245 Indian and foreign insurers in all.

By 1936, Ramkrishna had become widely recognized as an industrialist with factories and offices in several cities. He would acquire companies and businesses by purchasing shares and then using the managing agency system to manage and control them. With as little as a 4 per cent shareholding, Ramkrishna could effectively become the owner of a business.

A large part of his business empire's expansion came through acquisitions rather than setting up new factories from scratch. Among his peers, Ramkrishna was one of the few who grew their businesses exponentially using this route. Ramkrishna's background in speculation, deep knowledge of the stock market and extensive market network made it easier for him to acquire businesses. The fact that he had set up and was running sugar mills, paper mills and even chemical factories enhanced his standing in the business world. No longer was he seen merely as a speculator; he was regarded as a leading industrialist. In terms of wealth, he quickly rose to become one of the top businessmen of his time. A significant portion of his wealth continued to come from speculation, which he carried out in Calcutta. Due to the fact that he controlled the price of silver in the market, he was known as the 'Silver King'.

Ramkrishna maintained his association with the Indian National Congress, continuing to make financial contributions to the party and interacting with its leaders. Some of these leaders were given partnerships in the managing agencies of the various companies he acquired, ensuring their continued association with him.

Ramkrishna Takes on the Mighty ACC

By the early 1930s, Delhi was being developed as the capital of India. The British had shifted the capital from Calcutta to Delhi in 1911 during the Durbar—a grand event to welcome and celebrate King George V. However, the development of the new capital had been delayed due to the First World War. By the late 1920s and early 1930s, work to expand the city was progressing at full speed.

Ramkrishna, ever the astute investor, bought several bungalows in central Delhi.

One of his neighbours in Delhi was Muhammed Ali Jinnah. Ramkrishna had first met Jinnah as part of a group of political leaders. The two men were as different as could be. Jinnah, a British-educated lawyer and politician, was suave and worldly, enjoying non-vegetarian food, drinks and expensive cigars. Ramkrishna, on the other hand, was a devout Hindu who would sprinkle Ganga jal to purify a space if a Muslim had entered it. A strict vegetarian, he did not eat onions or garlic, nor did he drink tea or coffee. He was rustic, dressed entirely in khadi and was a home-grown industrialist. Even his most ardent well-wishers did not describe Ramkrishna as suave. It was astounding to the world that these two men became close friends. But they did. Opposites did indeed attract, it seemed.

Ramkrishna was able to devote time to his political associates as he had entrusted the running of the business to his brother and son-in-law. However, he remained engaged and was always on the lookout for new opportunities. One that caught his interest was the safe deposit and cold storage business.

National Safe Deposit and Cold Storage Ltd specialized in modern warehouses. It operated facilities in Calcutta, Lucknow and Kanpur. The warehouses had massive iron vaults and over 5,000 lockers of varying dimensions, which could hold valuables of all kinds, from jewellery to important documents. The lockers were protected against burglary, fire, earthquake, air raids, floods and more. The vaults were air-conditioned.

Ramkrishna acquired control of the company through the managing agency route. Very soon, the company was under the management of Dalmia-Jain Co. Ltd.

In 1935, Ramkrishna sought to enter the cement industry. Once he did, he got into a fight with one of the most powerful cement companies in India at the time—ACC.

India had entered the cement era in 1914 when a company in Porbandar, Gujarat, began manufacturing cement. The demand for cement was high, and even though it produced only one type—Artificial Portland Cement—the company was financially successful. At the time, most of India's cement came from England, and the price of this imported cement was high. The Indian market, with its advantage of cheap labour and ample raw material, attracted more entrants. Within a few years, two more companies set up cement plants, one in Madhya Pradesh and another in Rajasthan.

By the early 1920s, however, cement factories were operating at only 50 per cent of their capacity. What was surprising was that even at that low rate of production, supply still exceeded demand. To increase sales, the companies resorted to selling cement at prices well below production costs. As this practice was not financially viable in the long run, some companies were forced to liquidate and shut down operations.

At this point, the government intervened. It referred the working of the cement industry to the Tariff Board. After examining the matter, the Board recommended cooperation among the existing units as essential for their survival. This resulted in the formation of the Indian Cement Manufacturers

Association in 1925. The Association aimed to regulate prices and limit supplies in the market through mutual consent.

Subsequently, in 1927, members of the Association established the Concrete Association of India to promote the use of indigenous cement in construction materials. Three years later, in 1930, another association was launched to promote the sales and distribution of cement at regulated prices.

In 1936, eleven existing cement companies merged to form Associated Cement Companies Limited (ACC). The plan was formulated by Framroze Edulji Dinshaw, also known as Framji Dinshaw. He owned 12.5 per cent of Tata Sons, the holding company of the Tata Group. A top lawyer of his time and known for his sharp business acumen, Dinshaw devised the merger as a means of consolidating the industry. However, he died unexpectedly in 1936.

The plan might have been abandoned after Dinshaw's death, but Sir Nowroji Saklatvala stepped in. Saklatvala, an eminent figure related to Sir Jamsetji Tata and a trusted lieutenant of Sir Dorabji Tata, took it upon himself to find common ground among the conflicting interests in the cement industry. His efforts brought the merger to fruition, and ACC came into being. Saklatvala served as its first chairman.

At the time, the cement industry was not doing well. However, Ramkrishna, ever the speculator and risk-taker, reckoned that it would do very well in India in both the near and distant future. He began searching for a company to purchase and enter the industry but could find none. When he discussed the matter with Jaidayal and Shanti Prasad, they advised him to look at a new venture instead.

Ramkrishna agreed, but before proceeding further, he sought a meeting with Nowroji Saklatvala. The year was 1935, and the merger of the cement companies was not yet public knowledge.

Ramkrishna's reputation had grown significantly due to the many factories and businesses he owned. Even though he remained active in the satta market, he was no longer seen as only a speculator. Impressed by his stature, Saklatvala agreed to meet him.

Ramkrishna told Saklatvala that he wanted to establish a cement factory.

'But why do you want to set up a cement factory, Mr Dalmia? Don't you know the existing cement companies are in dire straits?' asked the suave Saklatvala. He was dressed in a three-piece suit and spoke impeccable English, while Ramkrishna was in his trademark khadi attire.

'Yes, I am aware of this, Sir Nowroji. But I am convinced that this industry is going to make great gains. India will need a huge amount of cement in the coming years, and I want to be part of that growth,' replied Ramkrishna with a broad smile.

Saklatvala looked at the younger man sitting before him, marvelling at his appetite for risk. Although he had heard stories of Ramkrishna's risk-taking and speculation in the market, he found it hard to reconcile all that he had heard with the demeanour of the man before him. Ramkrishna's outward simplicity gave no indication of his razor-sharp mind.

'Are you sure you want to enter the cement industry, Mr Dalmia? It is not an easy business, I must warn you,' Saklatvala said, trying once more to dissuade Ramkrishna.

'Yes, I am sure. Absolutely sure. But I must admit, I worry that if you set up more cement factories and compete, it will be difficult for me to survive. If that happens, I will not go ahead with my plans,' said Ramkrishna candidly. He saw no harm in letting Saklatvala know of his fears.

Saklatvala was impressed with Ramkrishna's frankness. He could not help but like the man before him.

'Mr Dalmia, this is a vast ocean. Anyone can use it. But we will not compete with you,' Saklatvala said, deciding in an instant to give Ramkrishna his word.

Knowing Saklatvala to be a man of integrity, Ramkrishna felt reassured and proceeded with his plan to open a cement factory.

The factory required machinery that was unavailable in India. The best equipment was manufactured in Germany and Denmark. Ramkrishna decided to send Jaidayal to Europe to source the machines.

At the time, Jaidayal was in his early thirties and had never travelled overseas. Further, the war had started, and the environment was uncertain. He was hesitant to travel to Europe, especially to Germany.

Unable to say no to his brother directly, Jaidayal took the easy way out. He went to the Brahmachari Prabhusantji Ashram in Allahabad without informing anyone in the family, hoping that in his absence, Ramkrishna would find someone else to go to Europe.

Ramkrishna was put in a spot when he discovered Jaidayal's absence. He realized that Jaidayal did not want to travel, but he was determined that Jaidayal go because he trusted him implicitly and knew he was knowledgeable about machinery. Ramkrishna began searching for Jaidayal's whereabouts. He spoke with many of his brother's friends, but no one knew where he was.

Finally, Ramkrishna remembered Mohan Lal Goenka, a close friend of Jaidayal's, and went to his house to meet him. At first, Mohan Lal was hesitant to speak about Jaidayal, but Ramkrishna soon put the young man at ease with his charming manner. Mohan Lal told Ramkrishna that Jaidayal was afraid of travelling alone to Europe and thus was hiding in the ashram.

Ramkrishna understood his brother's fear but remained firm in his decision that Jaidayal must go to Germany. Empathizing with his brother's reluctance to travel alone, he thought for a moment and then told Mohan that Jaidayal could take his wife, Krishna, and their son, Vishnu Hari, along with him. Mohan agreed that this was a good idea and believed it could help assuage Jaidayal's apprehensions.

Mohan promised Ramkrishna that he would go to Allahabad and persuade Jaidayal, but felt it would be better if someone else went along with him. He approached Hanuman Prasad Poddar.

Poddar was a well-known and highly respected man in society. He was the editor of *Kalyan*—a journal published since 1926—and a good friend of Ramkrishna. Poddar was also a mentor to Jaidayal.

After hearing out Mohan Lal's account, Poddar agreed that Ramkrishna was right to insist on Jaidayal travelling to Europe to buy the machines. He also concurred that having Krishna and Vishnu Hari accompany Jaidayal would help. He further suggested taking a servant along as well to help them during the journey and in Europe.

Armed with these suggestions, the two men left for Allahabad.

Jaidayal was surprised to see them at the ashram.

'What brings you here, Bhaiji?' he asked after touching Poddar's feet.

'And you, what are you doing here, my friend?' Jaidayal asked Mohan Lal as he hugged him tightly.

'Jaidayal, I understand that Ramkrishna wants you to go to Germany to procure the machines for the cement factory,' Poddar said, coming straight to the point.

Jaidayal looked at Poddar in amazement. Then he turned to Mohan Lal with raised eyebrows, silently asking a question. Mohan Lal nodded slightly, confirming that they knew of the matter.

'How do you know this?' Jaidayal asked, unable to believe that the two men had travelled to speak to him about a trip he did not want to take.

'I will be honest with you, Jaidayal. Ramkrishna was very worried when he couldn't find you. No one knew where you were. Your bhabhi, Durga, has been weeping since you went missing. Mohan here knew where you were and told Ramkrishna,' Poddar explained.

By then, Jaidayal had brought out some cane chairs for his visitors. Poddar settled into the comfortable chair and accepted the glass of water offered to him.

Jaidayal glared at Mohan Lal when he heard that it was his friend who had revealed his location. Poddar caught the angry look.

'Now, don't be angry, Jaidayal,' Poddar admonished his mentee lightly. He then gestured for the two younger men to sit down. They had been standing, and Jaidayal had been pacing nervously.

'Tell me, Jaidayal, is Ramkrishna doing anything that could harm you? In fact, let me rephrase that. Could Ramkrishna ever do anything to bring you harm, eh? Tell me,' asked Poddar, looking intently at Jaidayal.

Jaidayal could only shake his head. He knew that Ramkrishna loved him more than anyone else in the world and would never let any harm come to him.

'So, you agree that Ramkrishna is not sending you to Europe to harm you. Good. Now, tell me, you like working with machines, don't you? And don't you proudly tell anyone who'll listen that you understand machines better than anyone?' Poddar continued, asking questions to which he already knew the answers.

This time, Jaidayal nodded enthusiastically. It was true—he loved working with machines.

'So, why are you surprised that Ramkrishna wants you to go? You also know that he trusts you implicitly. For such an important project, he doesn't want to take any risks. That is why he wants you—and only you—to go. Can you not do this for your brother?' Poddar continued.

'But ... but ... I ... I ... ' stammered Jaidayal, hesitating. He could not refute any of the older man's arguments, yet, fear and hesitation lingered within him. He felt ashamed to articulate his fears, thinking it would make him seem weak.

Poddar noticed Jaidayal's hesitation. He did not want to embarrass Jaidayal and gestured for him to be quiet.

'Yes, yes, I know you must be worried about leaving your wife and young child behind,' Poddar tactfully redirected the reason for Jaidayal's reluctance.

Jaidayal realized that he was being handed a lifeline and latched on to eagerly.

'Yes, yes, Bhaiji, you are right. I am worried about Krishna. And Vishnu is young. I will not be able to concentrate on work if I am constantly thinking about them. That is why I don't want to go,' Jaidayal said in a rush, the words tumbling out.

'This problem is easily solved, Jaidayal. In fact, I told Ramkrishna that you cannot send your brother to Europe alone. Who will look after him there? He understood immediately and said that Krishan and Vishnu will also go with you,' said Poddar triumphantly, leaning back in his chair with a satisfied smile and a gleam in his eyes.

Jaidayal looked at his mentor and knew there were no excuses left.

'Bhaiji, I am ready to go. But there is no need for Krishna and Vishnu to come with me. What will they do there? It will be tough for them,' Jaidayal said, forgetting that they had been his excuse for not wanting to leave.

'No, no, no, Jaidayal. They are needed so you can eat properly. You know it's a foreign land, and you may not get the kind of food we all eat here,' Poddar chided.

'I am an adult, Bhaiji. I can look after myself. I can eat fruit and dry fruits and have plenty of milk and curds. I will manage. Let them stay. I will go alone,' Jaidayal said, now wanting to prove his courage.

'No, Jaidayal. Your wife and child will go with you. And I will ask Ramkrishna to send a servant as well so that none of you face any discomfort,' Poddar replied firmly, signalling that the discussion was over by rising from his chair.

Mohan Lal, who had remained silent until now, found his voice.

'It will be a good trip, Jaidayal. You will come back with many stories for all of us. We will be waiting to hear them,' he said, slapping his friend on the back. He was relieved that Poddar had solved the problem.

The matter was settled, and the party left for Germany on a steamer ship. The journey began in Bombay during the monsoon season. The sea was rough, and huge waves buffeted the ship, causing it to rock from side to side. Jaidayal, unaccustomed to the motion of the sea, suffered terrible seasickness. There were times he wished he could get off the ship and return to India, but of course, that was not possible.

It took three or four days for the ship to reach the calmer waters of the Red Sea. Jaidayal heaved several sighs of relief. Once he was better, he took stock of his family and found that they had not been as severely affected by seasickness. In fact, his son had not been affected at all. While Jaidayal had been bemoaning his fate and vomiting, young Vishnu Hari had been running around, exploring every corner of the ship. The ship's staff had taken to the child and Vishnu Hari had made friends with the stewards and other crew members.

Jaidayal's frequent vomiting had emptied his stomach thoroughly, leaving him hungry once the ship reached calmer waters. Unfortunately, the sweetmeats they had carried from Calcutta had spoiled. The humid sea air had caused them to turn mouldy, and they had to be thrown away.

Jaidayal had also purchased Alphonso mangoes in Bombay. During the initial days of the journey when they had been battling seasickness, the family had been unable to eat the mangoes. By the time the ship reached the Red Sea, the mangoes were in danger of over-ripening. To avoid wasting them, the family shared the mangoes with everyone, and the entire ship had a feast.

Krishna had carried an Icmic cooker with her so she could cook during the voyage.

The Icmic steam cooker, a precursor to the modern-day pressure cooker, was invented in the 1910s by Indumadhab Mallick in Calcutta. Indumadhab was a genius and a multifaceted man with postgraduate degrees in subjects as diverse as philosophy and physics, a Bachelor of Law degree, and a medical education from Calcutta Medical College.

Once, when on a pilgrimage to Puri with his family, he observed the temple's preparation of *mahaprasad*, or *anna Brahma*—a daily offering to the deity that included fifty-six delicacies cooked in the temple kitchens. The mahaprasad was given to the devotees after it was offered to the deity. This food was prepared for more than one lakh devotees daily, using earthen pots and firewood as fuel.

Indumadhab was curious about the seamless and systematic cooking process and wanted to uncover its scientific principles. After conducting numerous experiments in Calcutta, he invented the Icmic cooker. The name, an acronym, was derived from *ic* (pronounced *ik*) for 'hygienic' and *mic* for 'economic'.

The Icmic cooker resembled a tiffin carrier, comprising several bowls or containers stacked one on top of the other. Each container held ingredients—rice, pulses, vegetables, fish—along with the condiments and spices needed for each dish. The stack was lowered into a large cylinder with a charcoal stove below. Water was added to the outer chamber, and the cooker was sealed before lighting the stove. The resulting steam, trapped inside the sealed device, cooked the food inside the containers slowly—just like a slow cooker.

The moist environment of the Icmic cooker was ideal for cooking Indian food, making it a runaway hit in Bengali homes. Housewives could load the Icmic cooker and spend time away from the kitchen. As it was not pressurized, there was no risk of the cooker exploding. Additionally, since the food was cooked slowly, it tasted better.

Krishna had carried this Icmic cooker with her on the ship. However, she found it difficult to use it in the cabin due to the ship's rocking motion. Even when supported with other items, the cooker would topple over. Moreover, Jaidayal feared that the wooden cabin floor might catch fire if the burning charcoal spilled. He told Krishna to stop using the cooker.

This, then, led to the problem of what to eat and where to eat. The family did not like eating in the dining room as most of the passengers there ate non-vegetarian food. Being strict vegetarians, Jaidayal and Krishna felt nauseated even by the smell of meat. They took to eating in their cabin.

The waiters would serve them breakfast in their cabin, which included toast, various breads, butter, fruit, milk and honey. Initially, Jaidayal and Krishna ate what they wanted at breakfast and asked the waiter to clear the rest. However, they soon realized they felt hungry by 11 a.m., and as the kitchen was closed by then, they could not get anything to eat until lunch. So, they began keeping all the breakfast offerings. Whatever they didn't eat was saved and eaten whenever they felt hungry between meals.

Laundry presented another issue. Initially, they sent their clothes daily to the ship's laundry, as it was customary for them to change their clothes every day. Soon, however, Jaidayal saw that the laundry bill was ballooning. So, he instructed the servant to wash their clothes in the cabin bathroom, which then doubled as a dhobi ghat!

When the ship docked in Egypt, Jaidayal and his family disembarked, glad to feel terra firma beneath their feet. They were invited to the homes of a few Indian families, and Jaidayal accepted the invitations gladly. He was delighted to enjoy home-cooked Indian food after many days.

At Marseilles, the Dalmia family disembarked from the ship and took a train to Berlin. Ramkrishna had arranged a private, fully furnished apartment for Jaidayal and his family. However, the apartment had no provisions in the kitchen, and Krishna found it very inconvenient to go to the grocery store for every need. They were not accustomed to Western living, which was more structured than their lifestyle in Calcutta. Thus, they moved to a hotel.

Living in the hotel was comfortable, but food continued to be a problem. Krishna still had her Icmic cooker with her. Unable to eat the bland, mainly non-vegetarian food served in the hotel, she wanted to use the Icmic cooker to prepare meals in their room. Initially, the hotel staff opposed this. However, Jaidayal asked them if they wanted their guests to remain hungry. It worked. Permission was granted, but with a strict warning not to set anything on fire.

Realizing that the wooden floor of their room could be vulnerable to heat, Jaidayal asked the hotel staff for a table with a granite top. Once they had the table, the Icmic cooker was placed on it, and a small kitchen was set up in their room. The Dalmias were finally able to eat the food they liked.

The hotel charged the equivalent of Rs 200 per day for the premium, front-facing rooms. However, the rooms at the back of the hotel cost only Rs 60 per day. Knowing they would need to stay in Germany for a couple of months, Jaidayal asked the hotel to move them to the rooms at the back. They took two rooms—one for themselves and the other for meetings with the machinery manufacturers.

Vishnu, meanwhile, had made friends with the hotel staff. Just like the crew on the ship, the hotel staff took a liking to the young boy. Vishnu spent a large part of the day in the elevator, riding up and down with the liftman. He even learned the functions of various buttons in the elevator and picked up a smattering of German.

The Dalmia family enjoyed taking evening walks around the hotel. Although he had carried formal trousers and shirts with him, Jaidayal found them tedious to wear. He preferred his dhoti paired with a shirt, while Krishna wore saris. The locals, unaccustomed to seeing Indians, found them a novelty. Many would stare at them, and some even approached them to ask questions about their attire.

While Jaidayal and his family were in Berlin, Ramkrishna had been busy in India. After Jaidayal's departure for Germany, the consolidation of ten cement companies into the ACC was completed, with Nowroji Saklatvala as its first chairman.

Ramkrishna was furious. He felt that Nowroji had gone back on his word. However, a rational part of his mind reminded him that neither Nowroji nor the Tatas had set up a new cement factory. Instead, they had merely consolidated existing companies to form a giant enterprise.

Ramkrishna realized that his single cement factory would be a minnow compared to ACC, which would no doubt rule the market. Although the philosophy behind the merger was to prevent a monopoly-like situation in the market, Ramkrishna was certain that ACC would eventually function as a monopolistic organization.

Always a man to make swift decisions, Ramkrishna decided that instead of setting up just one cement factory, he would establish two large ones. He was still bullish on the future demand for cement.

He discussed his thoughts with his good friend Hanuman Prasad Poddar, whom he regarded as a brother and trusted completely. Ramkrishna, younger than Poddar by seven months, called him Bhaiji as a mark of respect. Poddar listened to Ramkrishna and agreed with his decision to set up more than one factory.

'Ramkrishna, if you want to set up more than one factory, you need to decide now,' counselled Poddar.

'Why, Bhaiji? Why do I need to make the decision immediately?' Ramkrishna asked, puzzled. While he liked to take quick decisions, he wondered why such urgency was necessary.

'See, Jaidayal is in Germany to buy the machinery. If you set up one factory now and then decide to set up another in six months, Jaidayal will have to repeat the journey and negotiations all over again. Why not decide now where you want to set up the factories and ask Jaidayal to negotiate for all the machines at once?' explained Poddar.

'That is a brilliant idea, Bhaiji. If we place an order for more machines, we will get a better rate. I can tell the suppliers that delivery dates will be decided later. I will call up Jaidayal and tell him to negotiate for more machines,' Ramkrishna said, excited as he saw the logic in Poddar's counsel.

Jaidayal had left India with instructions to buy machinery for a capacity of 200 tonnes per day. Ramkrishna called him and instructed him to negotiate for machinery with a capacity of 300 tonnes per day.

'But Bhaiji, I am already in negotiations, and the companies are working on estimates for 200 tonnes per day. Now you want 300 tonnes? Are you sure?' Jaidayal asked for clarity. He knew the European way of working was more structured than the Indian way, and changing specifications or requirements would mean starting the entire process from scratch.

'Yes, I am sure. Tell them you want a higher capacity. They will be happy as they are getting more business,' Ramkrishna said briskly, unable to understand why anyone would hesitate to accept a larger order.

Jaidayal went back to the companies and asked them to prepare estimates for a higher capacity. As expected, he was told it would take some time. While he was waiting, he received another phone call from his brother.

'Jaidayal, I want you to place an order for a capacity of 400 tonnes per day,' Ramkrishna said excitedly. He had done some calculations and decided to set up more factories.

'Bhaiji, please make up your mind. I have already changed the order from 200 to 300 tonnes per day. I have been in Germany for two months already. If we keep changing our minds, I will have to stay here permanently, which I do not want to do,' Jaidayal replied exasperatedly. He was irritated, as he was the one dealing with the foreigners, who took their time with everything. He did not want to keep changing the requirements.

'All right, just ask them for a capacity of 500 tonnes per day,' Ramkrishna said, raising the figure even further.

'Is this final, Bhaiji?' Jaidayal asked, wanting to be absolutely sure.

'Yes. Now go and get the best deal. Also, tell them we will provide the delivery schedule later,' confirmed Ramkrishna.

Jaidayal got to work. He had been speaking with FLSmidth, a Danish company that manufactured machines for producing cement. Commonly known as FLS, the company also had a representative office in India, and their machines were used by ACC.

Jaidayal wanted to widen his search as the order for machines would be substantial. Other companies were interested as well, eager to expand their customer base into India. The problem was that Jaidayal did not know enough about the machines to differentiate the advantages of one from the disadvantages of another. Before leaving for Germany, he had managed only an hour-long walkthrough of an Indian cement factory.

Jaidayal set up a telephone call with his brother, thinking it would be best to seek his advice on the matter.

When Ramkrishna heard about the problem, he burst out laughing.

'Why are you laughing, Bhaiji? Did I say something funny? Or are you laughing at me because I don't know enough about the machines?' Jaidayal asked, miffed. He felt he was in a tough spot and didn't appreciate his brother making light of it.

'Arrey, Jaidayal, not at all. I am laughing because you are worrying over nothing. The solution is so simple,' said Ramkrishna, still chuckling.

'How can it be simple? I am not an engineer, and it would take me years to study the machines in detail to figure out which ones are better,' Jaidayal countered, still seeing the problem as daunting.

'You do not need to study anything, my brother,' said Ramkrishna more seriously.

'Then how can I figure it out, Bhaiji? Please tell me, and stop laughing,' said Jaidayal as Ramkrishna started chuckling again.

'It's simple, my brother! Call the representative of one company and ask him the advantages of his machine. Then ask him how his machine is better than those of his competitors. He will tell you all the negative points about their machines while sharing all the good points about his own. Do this with every machine manufacturer. In no time at all you will have a detailed understanding of the positive and negative aspects of all the machines. After that, you are smart enough to figure out which ones are best for us,' explained Ramkrishna patiently.

'Bhaiji, what a wonderful idea! I am so glad I talked to you,' Jaidayal exclaimed, almost jumping with excitement. He was eager to go and find out all he could about the various machines.

Jaidayal did exactly as his brother had instructed. Sure enough, within a short time, he knew which machines he wanted to buy.

There were two types of machines for cement manufacture—one for the wet process and the other for the dry process. The wet process involves the use of water and a slurry of raw materials to create a cement paste. This past is then formed into a mould and is allowed to harden. The dry process, on the other hand, reduces the moisture content of the raw material to less than 1 per cent before the blending process begins. The dry material is pulverized and fed into a rotary kiln. Both processes have their own advantages and disadvantages. While the wet process makes grinding easier, the dry process saves on fuel costs.

At that time, cement plants in India primarily used machines for the wet process of cement production. However, Jaidayal opted for the dry process machines for the plant that was to be set up in Karachi as he knew that the transportation of coal for fuel would be expensive there. Thus, the dry process machines, which conserved fuel, would work well there. For the other plants, he ordered machines that used the wet process. The dry process machines were made in Germany and were available at a lower cost because Adolf Hitler's Germany was offering significant discounts to encourage exports. Jaidayal, a skilled negotiator, used the discount from the Germans as leverage to persuade the Danes to reduce their price for the wet process machines.

Jaidayal believed his work in Germany was complete and began preparing to return home. However, Ramkrishna had other plans. After a discussion with Shanti Prasad, they decided to expand their paper mill to increase duplex paper production. Ramkrishna told Jaidayal to buy machines for this new plant line. Knowing that Jaidayal lacked expertise with paper manufacturing machines, Ramkrishna sent a Bengali gentleman to Germany to assist him.

Ramkrishna also thought of setting up a paper mill at this time and asked Jaidayal to buy the machines needed. Paper was made from bamboo, and Dalmianagar, located in Bihar, was surrounded by dense bamboo forests. Many machines were available to crush bamboo. After evaluating several machines in Germany, Jaidayal decided to visit the UK. A.W. Smith, a company based in Glasgow, had provided machines for the sugar mill at Dalmianagar. Jaidayal thought the same machines could be used to crush bamboo. This paper mill would go on to earn crores for the Dalmias in later years.

The cement factories were to be established in Dalmianagar and Karachi. Ramkrishna put Shanti Prasad in charge of the Dalmianagar factory and sent Jaidayal to set up the Karachi plant.

Meanwhile, ACC had established its dominance in the Indian cement market. The clouds of war were gathering over the rest of Europe and the effects were felt in India as well.

However, Ramkrishna was unconcerned. He was looking ahead—perhaps to a world after the war, which was imminent. Always a risk-taker, he decided to take a bold step and take on ACC. He realized that just two cement plants would not be enough to challenge the might of ACC, so he resolved to set up four more.

He planned to establish cement plants across the country to better counter ACC in the market. He anticipated that ACC would drop their prices in areas where his plants were located, offsetting those losses by charging premiums in regions where ACC was the only cement company. To provide competition nationwide, he established plants in Dalmiapuram in the south, Dandot in Punjab, Charkhi Dadri in Haryana and another in Karachi.

The Dalmianagar and Karachi plants were set up first and started production. As Ramkrishna had anticipated, ACC dropped their prices in those regions. Dalmia Cement responded by lowering their prices as well. Ramkrishna waited for ACC to retaliate and soon realized he had an advantage over them.

ACC was a board-run company. If they wanted to drop prices in a region, neither the managing director nor the Secretary could sanction it alone—board approval was required. Further, a board meeting necessitated a minimum ten-day notice. At the meeting itself, decisions would be debated and argued, which caused delays in decision-making.

Ramkrishna, on the other hand, could make decisions in an instant. Once he decided on a price cut, Dalmia Cement dealers were immediately informed. Dealers who had purchased stock at higher prices were compensated in cash for the losses they would incur selling at the new lower prices. Ramkrishna realized that ACC could not do that as they had to follow a structured sales process and a board procedure.

Thus, every time ACC dropped their prices anywhere in India, Ramkrishna would lower his prices even further. To decrease their prices even more to stay competitive in the market, ACC had to go through the entire rigmarole of issuing a notice, holding a board meeting and then deciding on a rate cut. This took time and was tedious.

Once Ramkrishna understood this 'game', he would drop prices at a location immediately after an ACC board meeting was held. Dalmia Cement had plants in six locations across India, and he would employ this strategy unpredictably at each location. The erudite executives at ACC soon grew frustrated with this 'game' and wanted an 'understanding' or a settlement with the street-smart Ramkrishna.

Meanwhile, Ramkrishna had been purchasing a large number of ACC shares in the market. His plan was to acquire enough shares to demand a seat on ACC's board. He wanted to be in the lion's den itself. With no market regulator, there was no limit to the number of shares he could buy. However, the number of shares required for a board seat was substantial, and Ramkrishna could not buy them all at once. Thus, he acquired them whenever he could, buying outright at the prevailing price.

Ramkrishna had another reason for cornering ACC shares, tied to the share price itself. He bought more shares worth a few crores in the forward market. His reasoning was that if Dalmia Cement incurred losses, it would be ACC that would gain profits, driving up its share price. Since he had bought the shares at a lower price, he could sell them at the higher price and make a profit, offsetting his losses in the cement business.

He counted on ACC's share price going up, leading to large profits for him. However, events played out differently.

ACC became aware of Ramkrishna's forward trades. They decided to prolong the discussions for arriving at a settlement to end the market war between them and Dalmia Cement to stretch Ramkrishna financially. While negotiations over a market settlement were ongoing, ACC officials started dragging their feet. Further, the uncertainty around the war increased and the market fell. As Ramkrishna could not settle his forward trades, he was in serious financial trouble once again. The loss he would incur would be large enough to jeopardize his other brick and mortar businesses. He wanted discussions with ACC to proceed faster, but ACC officials knew they could let the matter drag.

Ramkrishna immediately approached Sir Akbar Hydari, a director at ACC and the prime minister of Hyderabad State, which owned a large number of ACC shares. Hydari, who was also working along with G.D. Birla to resolve the conflict between Dalmia Cement and ACC, advised Ramkrishna to meet the managing director of the Imperial Bank of India. The MD, a European, worked out of the bank's Bombay office. The Imperial Bank of India was the Treasurer of Hyderabad State.

Ramkrishna went to Bombay to meet the MD, but his troubles only increased. The MD, a prudent banker, upon hearing Ramkrishna's request, immediately called the bank's Calcutta branch to verify his standing. He was informed that Ramkrishna had an outstanding loan of Rs 10 lakh with the bank. The MD told Ramkrishna that he had to repay the loan immediately.

Ramkrishna was at a loss. He had gone to the MD expecting assistance, but the MD, seeing Ramkrishna's dire financial condition, wanted to safeguard the loan taken from his bank. Ramkrishna did not know what to do.

In this moment of crisis, he booked a telephone call to Poddar Bhaiji. Poddar heard Ramkrishna out but could not help him financially. He advised patience and urged Ramkrishna to keep faith in God.

Meanwhile, rumours of Ramkrishna's financial difficulties spread like wildfire. Other creditors became nervous. The Chartered Bank in Bombay demanded immediate repayment of their Rs 7 lakh loan. Ramkrishna realized he had to take matters in hand quickly or face financial ruin.

Ramkrishna turned to his maternal uncle, Motilal, the Silver King of Bombay, for help. He offered Motilal a share in the managing agency of Dalmia Cement. Motilal agreed to help his nephew.

Motilal was aware that the rumours flying around had damaged Ramkrishna's credit rating. Wisely, he took out loans against the physical shares held by Ramkrishna in his own name. Motilal knew that even if Ramkrishna were to use the shares as security, the market would not be willing to extend loans. Thus, he took the loans in his own name.

The immediate crisis was averted, but the cutthroat competition between ACC and Dalmia Cement continued in the market. Given Ramkrishna's longstanding support for the Congress and its leaders, he expected their help in settling the matter with ACC. He approached several top leaders, including Dr Rajendra Prasad, Subhash Chandra Bose and Sardar Patel, as well as industrialists such as Jamnalal Bajaj. However, none of them could persuade ACC to come to the negotiating table.

Jamnalal Bajaj, nonetheless, kept communication channels open with ACC executives. The company knew they were in pole position and were unwilling to make any significant compromises. What they were willing to do was consider a settlement if Ramkrishna sold his largest cement plant, located in Karachi, to them.

Initially, Ramkrishna was opposed to the idea. However, Jamnalal Bajaj, Jaidayal and Shanti Prasad sat with him for a long discussion. Shanti Prasad and Jaidayal pointed out that the fight with ACC was taking a toll on his health, and nothing was more precious than health. They advised him to sell the Karachi plant to ACC. Reluctantly, Ramkrishna agreed.

The next morning, Bombay newspapers ran bold headlines declaring, 'Dalmia Surrenders And Agrees To Sell His Factory To ACC'. Ramkrishna was furious. He was angry that the market saw his agreement as a surrender. It made him appear weak and small. He resolved to salvage the situation.

Ramkrishna approached Akbar Hydari and requested him to persuade the Nizam to purchase all the ACC shares he held. He offered them a price Rs 5 below the market rate, believing this move would instil confidence in the market. At the time, the Nizam was the seventh richest man in the world, known for his stables of racehorses at nearly every racecourse in India.

The Nizam, however, declined to purchase the shares in his personal name, as he had burnt his fingers financially by investing in mills owned by Gokuldas Mathradas. Nevertheless, since it was Akbar Hydari who had approached him, the Nizam hesitated to reject the proposal outright. Instead, he told Hydari to purchase a small quantity of the shares on the State's behalf.

Ramkrishna was happy but his relief was short-lived. Hydari, hesitant to take on too much risk, agreed to purchase only 25,000 shares at Rs 5 less than the market price. Ramkrishna had no choice but to accept.

The wily trader that he was, Ramkrishna returned to Bombay and divided the 25,000 shares into small lots. He distributed these to several brokers, instructing them to deliver these lots to the Imperial Bank on behalf of Hyderabad State.

The move created a buzz in the market. Brokers assumed that Hyderabad State had bought all of Ramkrishna's shares. Since each broker had a small lot, none of them could piece together the total number of shares sold, and they assumed Hyderabad State, and by extension the Nizam, had confidence in the company. This led to speculation that the price of ACC shares would rise.

There was a mad rush in the market to purchase ACC shares, causing their price to shoot up. Ramkrishna was ready for this. He held the remaining 1.25 lakh ACC shares with his friend and prominent broker, Sarup Chand Prithvi Raj. Within an hour, the broker sold the entire stock in the market, netting Ramkrishna a very handsome profit from the trade.

As soon as the market closed, Ramkrishna telephoned Jaidayal and told him not to allow any European experts from ACC to enter the Karachi factory. Word went back to ACC that Ramkrishna was preventing the factory inspection, which was the first step towards finalizing the sale. Sir Homi Mody, a key director of ACC (and Homi Mody was the father of the legendary Russi Modi, the head of Tata Steel), Homi Mody called Ramkrishna and asked him why was he going back on his promise.

'Which promise, Sir Mody?' asked Ramkrishna innocently.

'You had agreed to sell the Karachi factory to us, yet you are not allowing our European experts to enter the factory. It seems you no longer want to sell the factory. Isn't that breaking your promise?' said Homi Mody, clearly irritated.

'Sir Mody, I agreed to sell the factory, that's true. But we had not agreed on the sale price. Let us first discuss that. Once we agree on a price, then your experts can visit my factory any time,' said Ramkrishna.

He knew he was now in a position to demand a price so high that ACC would balk at agreeing to it.

Homi Mody realized he was beaten. Ramkrishna was right—the sale price had not been discussed, let alone agreed upon. ACC's senior directors were furious.

There were two reasons for their anger. One was the fact that the competition and cutthroat pricing would continue in the market. The second reason was that they resented being beaten at their own game by someone they considered an upstart. The ACC directors were sophisticated, British-educated, English-speaking men who dressed in sharp business suits. Ramkrishna, on the other hand, was a rustic, earthy man who had not completed his education and dressed in dhoti-kurta. Yet, there was little that ACC could do but continue the price war.

The market had been watching the battle between Ramkrishna and ACC with great interest. Known as a risk-taker in the market, Ramkrishna was now also recognized as an astute businessman. ACC was a monopolistic behemoth with an air of arrogance, while Ramkrishna was the underdog. The world loves an underdog, and many silently rooted for him. Once matters were settled, Ramkrishna was widely credited with breaking ACC's monopoly.

At this point, Ghanshyam Das Birla stepped in, offering to negotiate on Ramkrishna's behalf. G.D. Birla had been impressed by Ramkrishna's boldness in taking on the mighty ACC and winning the battle. He offered to mediate to bring about some order in the market. Purushottam Das Thakurdas, an industrialist of repute, represented ACC in the discussions. The negotiations went on for several weeks.

Fate, however, decided to intervene and settle matters. Even as discussions continued, the demand for cement surged due to the escalating war. ACC and Dalmia Cement no longer had to fight for market share; instead, they had to focus on maximizing production for the government.

Ramkrishna was crowned the 'King Slayer'. He was hailed for achieving what no other industrialist, big or small, had been able to do—taking on a giant like ACC and defeating them.

12
Ramkrishna Buys Times of India *Newspaper*

RAMKRISHNA was by now one of India's leading industrialists, with diverse business interests spanning sugar, cement, chemicals, glass, dairy, aviation, biscuits and more. He continued to play a role in the freedom movement, providing financial support to political leaders and the Congress party. He had acquired a taste for dabbling in politics and enjoyed the company of many political leaders including Gandhi, Subhas Chandra Bose, Rajendra Prasad, Sardar Patel and Nehru. His deep friendship with Jinnah also continued.

Ramkrishna had realized that together with his brother and son-in-law, they formed a formidable team. The two younger men left all financial decisions and acquisitions to Ramkrishna, recognizing his financial acumen. On their part, Jaidayal and

Ramkrishna Buys *Times of India* Newspaper

Shanti Prasad concentrated on managing the operations of their various enterprises, demonstrating their ability to run and oversee diverse businesses.

The business group, known as the Dalmia-Jain Group, had grown steadily in prominence and was counted among the biggest and best in the country.

In 1943, Ramkrishna established Bharat Bank. Ramkrishna decided almost overnight that he wanted to acquire the bank. The authorized capital of the bank was Rs 50 lakh, but in no time, Ramkrishna raised it to Rs 20 crore. He appointed new directors, including well-known individuals such as state chief ministers. Appointing political leaders as directors in his companies was a strategic way for Ramkrishna to oblige them. While he sometimes provided financial support directly, he found that offering directorships or partnerships in managing agencies was a more refined approach. The directors of Bharat Bank appreciated the prestige of their positions as well as the money they earned.

The bank soon expanded to 292 branches across the country. At the time, there was no centralized banking system, so each branch operated independently, catering to local markets and industries. Each branch had its own board, and Ramkrishna continued to appoint prominent individuals to these positions.

During the late 1930s and early 1940s, many British companies had seen the writing on the wall, realizing that India would soon gain its independence. Britisher owners therefore sought to sell their companies to local businessmen and industrialists and return to Britain. Ramkrishna saw a huge opportunity in this environment to acquire diverse companies. Being a risk-taker, he was willing to accepting losses in some ventures. Jaidayal and Shanti Prasad supported him.

The managing agency system allowed Ramkrishna to invest a small amount and acquire less than 10 per cent stakes in the companies he identified. Leveraging his network in the market and his growing reputation as an industrialist, he was able to get the shares of the acquired companies sold in the stock market.

The Dalmia-Jain Group went on an acquisition spree, securing a majority stake in three jute mills. Jute was a thriving industry in India at the time, and Andrew Yule managed three mills: Albion Jute Mills Ltd, Lothian Jute Mills Ltd and New Central Jute Mills Ltd. Ramkrishna bought a controlling stake in all three mills just before Independence. Some years later, the Group bought two more mills, this time in Bombay—Madhowji Dharamsi Manufacturing Co. Ltd and Sir Shapurji Broacha Mill Ltd.

By the end of the Second World War, the Dalmia-Jain Group forayed into the automotive sector. They purchased 50,000 American vehicles, including jeeps, weapon carriers and command cars. These war-used vehicles were repaired and reconditioned at the workshops of Allen Berry & Co. Ltd, a company Ramkrishna had acquired earlier.

Along with establishing his presence in the automotive sector, Ramkrishna expanded his aviation interests. Indian National Airways, that had been acquired during the pre-war years and had been part of Govan Brothers Ltd, continued to fly its planes. A new company, Dalmia-Jain Airways Ltd., was formed, which flew cargo planes. Ramkrishna's vision was to use these airlines to link up with other aviation companies and connect upcountry destinations with existing trunk routes.

Ramkrishna already had a presence in the railways sector, having previously acquired a small rail company for transporting raw materials to Dalmianagar. With his businesses now spread across the country, Ramkrishna expanded the railway company as well.

The business empire was growing, with the Dalmia-Jain Group continuing to acquire companies. Much of the momentum was due to Ramkrishna's trademark fast decision-making.

'How is it that you are able to take decisions so quickly, Pitaji?' asked Shanti Prasad one day, amazed by the speed at which his father-in-law processed information and analysed the viability of a business.

'I really don't know, son. Maybe it is God given, or perhaps it is something I developed during my years in the speculation business, where every minute—no, every second—is important. I think I unconsciously honed this skill during those days. But, I also think it is instinctive,' Ramkrishna replied after a moment's reflection.

Shanti Prasad nodded in understanding. He had seen his father-in-law in action and realized that this ability was not something that could be learnt over time.

'You know that every minute, nay, every second is important when speculating. So, I think I have unconsciously developed this skill,' Ramkrishna continued. He spoke slowly as if reflecting and getting the answer from within.

'That makes sense, Pitaji,' he agreed.

'My advice to you, son, is to make quick decisions. Decide as quickly as you can. And don't worry about making wrong decisions. Not all your decisions will be correct—maybe eight out of ten will be right—but the gains from those eight decisions will usually outweigh the losses from the two wrong ones,' advised Ramkrishna. In the absence of a son of his own, he regarded Shanti Prasad as one.

'I will remember this, Pitaji,' promised Shanti Prasad solemnly.

By the mid-1940s, the Dalmia-Jain Group, under Ramkrishna's leadership, had acquired a wide range of businesses. They owned several collieries, including Kharkhari Coal Co. at Junnardeo in the Central Province, Maheshpur Collieries Ltd in Jharia and Bharat Collieries Ltd, which had mines in Jharia, Barabani and Raniganj.

Besides these, the Group had several other companies, including Patiala Biscuit Manufacturers Ltd, located in the state of Patiala. It produced biscuits and a range of other food products. Ramkrishna also acquired Lesco Chemical Works Ltd, which manufactured pharmaceutical products in Kanpur. The Group had a presence in the chemicals sector through Dhrangadhra Chemical Works in Kathiawar, Gujarat, which produced soda ash and sodium bicarbonate. It also owned Rampur Distillery & Chemical Works Ltd, which utilized molasses from the sugar mills to manufacture spirits and liquors.

There was more. Rampur Maize Products produced glucose, starch and similar food products, while Shevaroy Bauxite Products Ltd, based in Yercaud, dealt in bauxite, emery and grinding paste.

With its presence in various industrial sectors and locations across the country, the Dalmia-Jain Group was the third-largest business conglomerate in India. Only the Tatas and the Birlas were bigger. Yet, despite managing such a wide variety of businesses and factories, Ramkrishna had set his sights on one more sector—he aspired to enter the media industry.

Ramkrishna held strong views on various aspects of politics and on cow protection. He had observed the influence newspapers wielded over public opinion, especially during his fight with ACC. He had already been funding the *National Herald* newspaper since its launch in 1938. The newspaper was founded by Jawaharlal Nehru, who served as its editor and chairman of its board.

At the newspaper's inception, *National Herald* was in need of funds. Mohanlal Saxena, a close associate of Nehru, approached Ramkrishna to sell shares of the newspaper. Ramkrishna had agreed and asked how much money was required. Saxena explained that even if he bought shares worth Rs 5,000 and gave them only 25 per cent of the money (Rs 1,250), it would be enough to meet the newspaper's immediate needs. After listening to Saxena, Ramkrishna decided to buy shares worth Rs 25,000 and assured him that he would pay the full amount within ten days.

Ramkrishna also nominated Shanti Prasad as a director on the *National Herald*'s board. Even after many years, the Jain family continued to hold 25,000 preferential shares of the newspaper. Through this, Ramkrishna became a significant shareholder of the *National Herald*. He had seen the critical role the newspaper played in shaping public opinion, especially in the fight for freedom.

Inspired by this, Ramkrishna decided that he, too, wanted to own a newspaper. He firmly believed that he could better serve his country by having a platform to reach millions of Indians. A newspaper, to his mind, was the best way to achieve this.

As he scouted the market, Ramkrishna identified the *Statesman* as a potential newspaper to buy. He held several meetings with the publication's editorial team. These meetings were not conducted in secrecy, and soon, word spread that Ramkrishna, once a speculator in the satta bazaar, had ambitions of owning of a respected, blue-blooded newspaper. The British owners of the publication developed cold feet, fearing that their brand's reputation would be compromised under an Indian owner, particularly someone like Ramkrishna. The deal fell through.

Although upset, Ramkrishna did not waste time brooding over the setback. During his discussions with the *Statesman*, he had befriended its chief editor, Sir Arthur Moore. Ramkrishna liked the Englishman, believing he had the right attitude. After the deal with the *Statesman* fell through, Ramkrishna requested Arthur to help him find another newspaper to acquire. Sir Arthur Moore agreed to leave the *Statesman* and work for Ramkrishna on a retainership basis.

Ramkrishna soon set his sights on *The Times of India*, which was published from London. Founded in 1838 as *The Bombay Times and Journal of Commerce*, the newspaper initially served the British residents of western India. It started as a biweekly publication and became a daily in 1851. Ten years later, in 1861, the newspaper changed its name to the now well-known name, *The Times of India*.

In 1892, Thomas Jewell Bennett and Frank Morris Coleman set up a joint stock company in Britain, named Bennett, Coleman & Company Limited, and acquired *The Times of India*. The company thrived, employing over 800 people. The newspaper had substantial circulation both in India and

Europe. Known for its editorial independence, *The Times of India* had gained national prominence by resisting frequent attempts by the government, business interests and cultural spokesmen to change its editorial policies.

It was this prestigious newspaper that Ramkrishna wanted to buy. He knew it would become the jewel in his crown. Acquiring a respected publication like *The Times of India* would enhance the prestige of the Dalmia-Jain Group as well.

Ramkrishna was cautious this time. He did not want a repeat of the fiasco with the *Statesman* to occur with *The Times of India*. He knew that any public disclosure of his intentions would make the deal a non-starter. Therefore, Ramkrishna dispatched Arthur Moore to London to work on the acquisition of the newspaper, instructing him to exercise the utmost discretion.

The Englishman spent several months in London at Ramkrishna's expense. Meanwhile, Ramkrishna's brother and son-in-law could not understand his obsession with owning a newspaper.

'Pitaji, this Arthur has been in London for a long time. He keeps sending us bills, and we have to keep paying them. Why do you want to buy a newspaper?' asked Shanti Prasad as the two men sat together at home one evening.

'Shanti Prasad, you do not understand the power of a newspaper. It can be the greatest weapon—no less than an atom bomb,' said Ramkrishna passionately.

'How so, Pitaji?' asked Shanti Prasad again. He could not fathom how a newspaper could equate to an atom bomb.

'Let me explain, son,' said Ramkrishna eagerly. 'You know, Shanti Prasad, that for us Indians, the morning hours are sacrosanct and precious. They are meant for intellectual and spiritual pursuits, for meditation and prayer. But look around you. The habit of reading newspapers has taken root among the educated class,' explained Ramkrishna.

'That is true, Pitaji,' Shanti Prasad agreed, nodding. 'Even I like to read the newspaper in the morning.'

'You see! I am right, am I not?' said Ramkrishna, delighted that his beloved Shanti Prasad agreed with him.

'And now that we agree the habit of reading the newspaper has taken root, let me tell you what happens. Without even attending to our morning ablutions, we all turn to news items, many of which contain untruths and propaganda,' Ramkrishna continued with passion.

Shanti Prasad nodded again in agreement.

'The object of purifying ourselves—not only physically but also mentally and spiritually—through prayers is to prepare ourselves for the day, which is influenced by the ideas imbibed in the morning. But these days, we are subject to the demoralizing effect of the newspapers' contents. Throughout the day, we judge events with bias and prejudice,' Ramkrishna said, speaking from the heart.

'Yes, Pitaji, but if you are against reading newspapers in the morning, why do you want to buy one?' asked Shanti Prasad, now thoroughly perplexed.

'I will tell you why, son. But first, let me also tell you this—people are prone to believe the newsman more than any other person, however responsible and respectable they may be. Sometimes we find that much of the news is untrue, yet the following day, we again believe in the veracity of the newspapers. Such is the tremendous influence the press commands over people these days,' explained Ramkrishna.

'Now let me explain why I want to buy a newspaper,' Ramkrishna said, finally coming to the point.

Shanti Prasad leaned forward in anticipation.

'The only remedy for all that is happening is for someone with courage to come forward and publish a paper that presents only the unvarnished facts, refraining from criticism or propagating any party's theory. It should instead appreciate the positives in each, as everybody possesses some goodness. Such a newspaper should serve the people earnestly,' said Ramkrishna with conviction.

'Ah! Pitaji, you want to bring out such a paper!' Shanti Prasad exclaimed in a eureka moment.

'Yes, son. You see, newspapers have their advantages too. They are immensely useful in educating the masses. Due to scientific inventions, happenings in one part of the world become known to the others in no time at all. Events in distant places, which earlier would not have been known for years—or even a lifetime—are now made known immediately,' Ramkrishna continued to explain.

'Pitaji, I now understand your need to buy a newspaper,' Shanti Prasad said, finally seeing the logic.

'I am not finished, young man. I have some more thoughts on how to run a newspaper,' said Ramkrishna briskly. He was talking about his favourite subject and wasn't going to let his appreciative audience of one slip away.

'Do tell me, Pitaji. These are valuable ideas,' said Shanti Prasad.

'We could develop a proper system for training journalists. It would go a long way in maintaining the reputation of the Fourth Estate. What newspapers need today is a cadre of trained and responsible journalists. There should be stringent laws in place so that only those journalists who have passed a specific test are qualified to work as editors, subeditors or even press reporters. Just as auditors cannot audit the accounts of registered companies without being properly qualified and recognized, the same should apply to journalists,' Ramkrishna said, clearly having thought deeply about the newspaper business.

'Pitaji, I am convinced. Let me get in touch with Arthur to find out the status of his negotiations,' Shanti Prasad said, now equally excited.

Ramkrishna immediately looked around and placed his index finger on his lips.

'Sshhhhhh, Shanti Prasad. This must be done in complete secrecy. If anyone gets even a whiff of it, the whole deal could be called off. You know how the English dislike selling their businesses to us Indians,' Ramkrishna said softly, as if afraid the walls were listening.

'Understood, Pitaji,' Shanti Prasad said, standing up and giving a mock salute to Ramkrishna.

Shanti Prasad and Ramkrishna emphasized the urgency of the matter to Arthur Moore. Finally, after several months, Arthur was able to convince the managing director of *The Times of India*, Sir Pearson, to come to India.

Sir Pearson and Ramkrishna met at the latter's home, where they discussed Bennett Coleman at length. Their conversation became so animated that later Ramkrishna's daughter asked him about it.

'Bapu, who was that Englishman? Why was he arguing with you about money?' asked his daughter.

Ramkrishna Buys *Times of India* Newspaper

'Yes, even I heard you two arguing in the round room,' agreed the mother.

'Oh, he was from Bennett Coleman. We were talking business,' said Ramkrishna hurriedly as he walked away.

The two women looked at each other, perplexed.

'Bennett Coleman? Who or what is Bennett Coleman?' asked one.

The other could only shake her head as she, too, did not know.

After a short time and many rounds of discussions at home, Ramkrishna finally reached an agreement with Sir Pearson regarding the purchase price. Pearson proposed that the two of them travel to Bombay, where *The Times of India* was headquartered.

While in Bombay, Sir Pearson became emotional.

'You want to snatch my baby away from me?' he said, referring to *The Times of India*. 'I have nursed it for over forty years, you know. And now you want it,' Pearson continued.

Ramkrishna looked at Pearson and reached out to pat his hand in a gesture of solace.

'Sir Pearson, the baby needs two nurses instead of one. It will thrive and be healthier,' said Ramkrishna.

Sir Pearson smiled but then tried another approach.

'So, Mr Dalmia, you really want to spend all that money to buy this? Are you truly ready to pay Rs 2 crore?' he asked, a gleam in his eyes.

Ramkrishna did not reply. Instead, he pulled out his chequebook. Opening it, he tore out a cheque, placed it on the table and signed it. He then handed the blank signed cheque to Pearson.

'Sir Pearson, although we agreed on this amount, here is the cheque. Please fill in any figure you wish. But I want *The Times of India*,' said Ramkrishna firmly.

'Are you mad, Mr Dalmia? You're trusting me with a blank signed cheque?' Pearson asked, flabbergasted. He could not believe that an Indian would hand over a blank cheque to an Englishman.

'Look at the generosity of us Indians, Sir Pearson,' Ramkrishna replied with a smile. He knew his dream of owning a newspaper was about to come true.

The deal was struck at Rs 2 crore, and in less than twenty-four hours, the ownership of *The Times of India* changed hands. The acquisition surprised all the prominent industrialists of the time. It was believed that a paper like *The Times of India* would not be available even to Europeans, let alone Indians.

The chief editor of the newspaper was Sir Francis Loe. Ramkrishna worked with him to revamp the newspaper. He also started the Delhi edition of *The Times of India*. His brother and son-in-law were against this expansion, as they believed it served no real purpose. However, Ramkrishna was resolute. His vision was to make *The Times of India* a world-renowned publication and the leading newspaper in the country. He believed that if the paper remained confined to Bombay, it would never achieve the reach he desired. (Today, *The Times of India* has fifty-five editions and is the largest-selling English newspaper in the world.)

Ramkrishna held strong views on politics, political leaders and society at large. Now that he had a newspaper, he had found a forum to air his opinions on a national scale. He was already a large shareholder in the *National Herald*, having invested Rs 25,000 in it and contributing a monthly amount for its operations. Now, he also acquired the *Civil and Military Gazette* of Lahore, which had a large circulation in Lahore and Karachi.

Ramkrishna used the newspaper to voice his political and social views. It was some of these views, published in his own newspapers, that would later land him in trouble.

13

Family Life and the Quest for a Son

DURING the years that Ramkrishna, along with Shanti Prasad and Jaidayal, was focused on expanding his business empire, he began to feel the absence of a son, especially as he reached his mid-forties. The longing intensified after Jaidayal and Krishna had their own sons, with Jaidayal's eldest, Vishnu Hari, born in 1924.

Ramkrishna, a deeply spiritual man, believed that he would not attain moksha unless he had a son. Though he treated Shanti Prasad like his own, his deep desire was to have a biological son. His wife, Durga, continued to be in frail health, and it was clear she could not bear another child. Ramkrishna was in a quandary. The prevalent law permitted a man to have multiple wives concurrently, but at heart, Ramkrishna was not in favour of a man marrying more than one woman. The lack of a son caused him considerable internal turmoil.

Life for Ramkrishna, however, was busy and did not allow him to dwell on this internal conflict and his quest for a son. Besides the businesses he was setting up, he was also deeply involved in the politics of the country. As a staunch supporter of the Congress party, he believed it was his duty as a businessman to provide the necessary backing to leaders in their fight for India's freedom.

By the late 1930s, Ramkrishna was known as a successful industrialist who had proved his mettle in the market. His standing grew significantly after his fight with ACC, where in the eyes of the market, the victory was his. Ramkrishna was also climbing the ladder of wealth and was recognized as one of the wealthiest men in India.

Political leaders gravitated towards Ramkrishna. For one, they needed his support, especially financial backing. Few industrialists or businessmen openly supported the Congress party, fearing the wrath of the British government. Ramkrishna, on the other hand, made a point of openly aligning himself with the party.

Another reason for Ramkrishna's appeal to Congress leaders was his personality. He was wiry, of slight build, dark-skinned and dressed in a crisp dhoti-kurta and white *topi*. He had an endearing personality and could connect with anyone on their level. His mind was sharp, and his convictions were even stronger. When he believed in a cause, he threw his full weight behind it, even at the risk of angering others.

Ramkrishna's motive for supporting political leaders had a self-serving aspect as well. A shrewd and street-smart businessman, he believed that providing financial support to politicians was, in a way, creating an opportunity for a 'payback' when the country became independent. He anticipated that political leaders, once in power, would offer help and support to his business interests.

Ramkrishna was also a staunch supporter of cow protection. He believed that the cow was a sacred animal. Before eating himself, he would always feed a cow first. He wanted a complete ban on cow slaughter, which he viewed as brutal and violent. Ramkrishna spoke to Gandhi about the issue. While Gandhi agreed that the practice was undesirable, he refused to advocate for a complete ban. Gandhi was focused on the political struggle for Independence and did not want the issue of cow slaughter to distract from the larger movement.

Ramkrishna was upset by Gandhi's refusal and wrote to him multiple times, urging him to take a firm stand. He knew that if Gandhi raised the issue of banning cow slaughter, the general public would support him. However, Gandhi remained firm in his decision.

Ramkrishna decided to take on the cause himself and launched the Anti-Cow Slaughter League in the 1940s. He himself gave up wearing leather shoes. Instead, he wore shoes made of soft cloth, custom made for him. He also avoided using silk for his shoes or clothing, as he believed in non-violence and knew that silk production involved killing many silkworms.

Busy as he was, Ramkrishna still yearned for a son. At times, he was able to ignore the deep longing; at other times, he allowed himself to think about having his own son.

He cared deeply for Durga, but he knew her health did not allow her to bear another child. The only option, he concluded after much deliberation, was to marry again. This was a difficult decision for Ramkrishna, as he had always been opposed to polygamy. In the mid-1930s, he had heard about a relative, Nagarmal Seksaria—the son-in-law of Jawala Prasad

Bhartiya—who, despite being married, wished to marry again. Ramkrishna had rushed to Lahore and used all his powers of persuasion to stop Nagarmal from committing polygamy. Thus, it was after a lot of internal turmoil that Ramkrishna decided that he needed to marry again if he wanted a son. The longing for a son ultimately overrode all his doubts.

Polygamy had been a longstanding practice in India and was legal until 1955 when the Hindu Marriage Act outlawed it.

Thus, the law was not a problem for Ramkrishna; it was his own sense of guilt. He knew that no woman would welcome her husband bringing home another wife. However, he reasoned that no wife would want her husband to be unhappy either. He did want a son, especially as he saw Jaidayal's sons growing up in the house. Ramkrishna also knew that if he sought his mother's permission, she would not grant it. So, he decided not to discuss his thoughts of remarriage with her at all.

Instead, he spoke with Durga about his dilemma. Durga, a simple-hearted and compassionate woman, was also a wife of her time. Women of that era were brought up to believe it was their duty to obey their husbands. Durga, too, believed it was her role to support her husband's wishes. She was also grateful to Ramkrishna for the care he had shown her, especially given her frail health since the early years of their marriage. She knew that in the absence of proper care, she would not live long, and once she was gone, Ramkrishna would be free to remarry, this time to a girl capable of bearing many children.

Durga had also witnessed the anguish Ramkrishna went through whenever his desire for a son raised its head. She could not bear to see her husband in such torment.

She agreed and told Ramkrishna that he could marry again.

However, Ramkrishna's friends were not as supportive as his own wife. Once he had Durga's approval, Ramkrishna felt confident enough to speak to his close friends about his decision to remarry. His friends, all married and with children, including sons, understood Ramkrishna's longing for a son yet advised against remarriage.

'But what is the way out? I cannot have a legitimate child unless I have a wife. And my wife is in delicate health. The doctors have told her she cannot have another child. Am I not allowed to attain moksha?' Ramkrishna asked sullenly.

He was sitting with his friend Jamnalal Bajaj, with whom he often discussed both business and personal matters.

'That is all true Ramkrishna, but you have to think of Durga as well,' said Jamnalal, who considered himself close enough to Ramkrishna to contradict him.

'I have already spoken with Durga, so don't worry,' Ramkrishna replied, waving off the objection.

'How can she disagree with you to your face, Ramkrishna?' asked Jamnalal shrewdly.

'Oh, you don't know my Durga. She can tell me whatever she wants,' Ramkrishna said with a hint of pride. He was proud of his wife.

'I still don't believe it. Let me speak to her myself,' Jamnalal persisted, unwilling to give up.

'You want to speak with her alone?' Ramkrishna asked, suddenly feeling protective of his wife.

'Arrey Ramkrishna, don't worry. I will take Subrata Devi with me. You know her, don't you? She is part of the famous Ruia family of Bombay,' Jamnalal reassured his friend.

'Ah yes! Subrata Devi, I know her. Very well, you can speak to Durga,' agreed Ramkrishna magnanimously. He was sure of his wife. He knew that, like him, once Durga made up her mind, she stuck to it.

Jamnalal Bajaj and Subrata Devi met with Durga. They sat down and broached the topic of Ramkrishna's desire to marry again.

'I know about it, Sethji', said Durga demurely, adjusting her pallu.

'But how can you agree to this?' asked Subrata Devi incredulously. She reached out and took Durga's hand in hers in a gesture of moral support.

'Behen, you know that a man cannot attain moksha without a son. Look at me', she said, gesturing to herself and her frailty. 'You know I cannot have any more children. Why should my husband be deprived of a son?' she continued, her voice soft but firm.

'But Durgaji, you are digging your own grave. Any new wife of Shri Dalmia will turn you out. After all, which woman is happy sharing her husband? And she will be younger than you as well', Jamnalal added, voicing his concerns.

Durga listened to Subrata Devi and Jamnalal patiently. Then she adjusted her pallu and folded her hands.

'My life is to serve him. I know he will not let me down. And even if he does not look after me, I know my brother-in-law, Jaidayal, will ensure I have two meals a day and four sarees a year', said Durga, her eyes steady and resolute as they met those of the two visitors.

Subrata Devi listened in amazement. She, too, folded her hands and bowed her head.

'Even if I were to surrender all my wealth at your feet, it would not compare to your unique qualities. You truly are a woman of lofty character,' said Subrata Devi. This time, it was Durga who patted the other woman's hand.

Jamnalal and Subrata Devi continued to have misgivings about Ramkrishna remarrying. They also understood that it was Durga's permission that was giving Ramkrishna the confidence to pursue his plan. They had tried to persuade Durga to reconsider her decision but had failed. They believed there was only one person who could convince Durga to change her mind.

Jamnalal and Subrata Devi invited Ramkrishna and Durga to accompany them to Wardha, where Gandhi was staying at the time. They hoped that Gandhi, who was against polygamy, could persuade Durga to change her mind.

However, even Gandhi could not sway Durga from her conviction. He advised her not to support Ramkrishna's plan to remarry. Durga listened, then folded her hands and bowed her head in front of Gandhi.

'Bapu, my life is to obey him,' she said simply.

Now that Ramkrishna had Durga's approval, he spoke to his mother about his decision. As expected, she was not happy with it. However, as was the norm in those days, she had no choice but to agree.

Once news of Ramkrishna's intent to remarry spread, many proposals started coming in. There were several offers from the fathers of young and beautiful women. However, Ramkrishna wanted to marry an educated woman who was older and could match him intellectually. He knew that beauty would fade with time, but an educated mind would only grow sharper. Furthermore, he was pragmatic enough to recognize that marrying a much younger girl at his comparatively older age could carry the risk of her going astray. By this time, Ramkrishna was in his late forties.

As part of his travels, Ramkrishna visited many ashrams. One such ashram in Ferozepur was run by Sant Takhat Singh. It was an ashram for girls, where over 1,500 girls received an education. Sant Takhat Singh also took on the responsibility of arranging marriages for these girls. During one of his speeches at the ashram, Ramkrishna noticed a beautiful girl. He later discovered that she was Sant Takhat Singh's daughter, Pritam. His earlier resolve not to marry a younger woman went flying out of his mind as he was smitten by her beauty. He believed that, being Sant Takhat Singh's daughter, she would have homely values.

Ramkrishna decided to marry Pritam. As with many of his decisions, this one too was made in an instant. Though she was much younger than him, he was undeterred and proposed to her directly. Durga, if she had any misgivings, did not express them in either word or action. Instead, she facilitated the marriage ceremony herself in Delhi in 1942.

However, after the marriage, Ramkrishna discovered that Pritam was a young girl with a strong and independent mind. She refused to conform to what she felt was his orthodox regime. In fact, she did not want to live with Ramkrishna and insisted on having her own house. She even refused to adopt his surname, choosing instead to retain her father's name. She continued to be known as Pritam Takhat Singh.

The marriage was short-lived. The ostensible reason for remarriage had been Ramkrishna's quest for a son, but with Pritam refusing to live with him, that purpose became moot. Eventually, the couple mutually agreed to separate without a formal divorce. Ramkrishna provided her with a substantial alimony and continued to look after her financial interests throughout her life. She went overseas and lived her life there. Ramkrishna was back in the market on the lookout for a wife.

M.B. Singh was a civil servant based in Lucknow. Among his children was a daughter named Saraswati. In her mid-twenties, Saraswati had already made a name for herself in the academic world. She had studied at the prestigious Isabella Thoburn College for Girls in Lucknow, studying Sanskrit, English and political science. Some acquaintances of Ramkrishna told him about Saraswati and her accomplishments.

Without even meeting her, Ramkrishna was impressed by Saraswati's academic achievements. He sent word to M.B. Singh, expressing his desire to meet his daughter and made it clear that his interest was matrimonial. By 1943, Ramkrishna was recognized as one of the leading industrialists in the country and was regarded as a 'catch' by any father seeking a suitable match for his daughter. M.B. Singh was no exception; he immediately invited Ramkrishna to Lucknow.

Ramkrishna accepted the invitation but chose not to meet Saraswati at her residence. Instead, he invited M.B. Singh and Saraswati to his home. Most prospective husbands at the time wanted to know about a girl's domestic skills, especially her abilities in the kitchen and whether she could care for her mother-in-law. Ramkrishna was different. He engaged in an intellectual discussion with Saraswati. Though initially intimidated by his personality, Saraswati was soon drawn into the conversation. M.B. Singh was a mere spectator and observed the discussion with great interest. He was to later tell friends that the interaction resembled a professor testing the knowledge of his student.

Ramkrishna returned to Delhi elated after his meeting with Saraswati, convinced that he had found his soulmate. He continued to meet her frequently, and Saraswati, too, developed an attraction for him.

Physically, Ramkrishna may not have been the most handsome man However, he had a magnetic personality. It seemed as though he knew he had to compensate for his average looks with above-average charm. His ability to connect with people enabled him to make friends easily. He had a deep voice, a charming smile, and people were captivated by his oratory skills. Thus, it was not difficult to understand how Saraswati, a young woman of twenty-six, developed feelings for a man more than twenty years her senior.

Ramkrishna and Saraswati married in 1943, almost a year after they had met. And in no time, Saraswati was pregnant. Ramkrishna was delighted. Interestingly, Rama, his only child until then, was almost the same age as Saraswati.

Saraswati had studied Sanskrit and Vedanta, and Ramkrishna shared her passion for both. While she was pursuing her master's degree, Saraswati had served as the chief editor of two university magazines, one in Hindi and the other in Sanskrit. Now, as a married woman with a husband of considerable means, Saraswati wanted to institute an award to promote both languages. She broached the topic with Ramkrishna, suggesting an award for outstanding literary works in Hindi. She believed it would go a long way in encouraging writers and academicians to produce better work.

'I like this suggestion, Saraswati. What a brilliant idea. Let us go ahead with it,' Ramkrishna agreed immediately.

'You really like the suggestion?' asked Saraswati hesitantly.

'Yes, of course. What is there not to like? So, when can you start working on it?' asked Ramkrishna briskly, waving off any hesitation on his wife's part.

'Who, me?' asked Saraswati in amazement, looking at her husband wide-eyed.

'Who else, Saraswati?' replied Ramkrishna, irritated by her lack of confidence.

'But how can I do it? I am not sure I'm capable of handling such a huge responsibility,' said Saraswati, still uncertain.

'Nonsense. Of course you can do this. Even with your pregnancy, you will have enough time and energy to devote to this. Didn't you yourself tell me that you were the chief editor of two university magazines? Now get going,' said Ramkrishna firmly, ending the discussion as he got up and left the room.

Saraswati continued to sit, gazing at her husband retreating back. Then, with a large smile, she stood up, her mind made up.

Saraswati quickly set to work, doing the groundwork for establishing the award. She was determined to elevate it into a prestigious and highly coveted award, recognized across the country. She reasoned that one key to enhancing its stature would be the people associated with it—those on the advisory committee and the chair of the award committee.

She spoke with Ramkrishna, and both agreed that Dr Rajendra Prasad, an eminent academician, would be the ideal chair of the committee. As Rajendra Prasad was a close friend of Ramkrishna, he promised to speak with him.

Two other distinguished personalities, Dr Amarnath Jha and Dr Pannalal, were invited to be members of the committee. They accepted the invitation immediately, partly because of Dr Rajendra Prasad's involvement.

With the committee and selection criteria in place, Saraswati wanted the award to reflect the legacy of her husband and his family. She suggested naming it the Harjimal Dalmia Award. Ramkrishna agreed at once.

The Harjimal Dalmia Puraskar was established in 1943 to honour the best Hindi writer of the year. The award soon became known as one of the most prestigious awards for Hindi writers. In fact, Durga and Rama used this award as inspiration to establish the now world-famous Jnanpith Award for literature.

The responsibilities associated with the award kept Saraswati busy, and she worked throughout her pregnancy. In 1944, Ramkrishna had his second child, a daughter whom they named Ila. While Ramkrishna loved his daughter, his desire for a son grew even stronger. Much as he cared for Saraswati, he reasoned that he needed another wife who could give him a son.

Sir P.C. Chatterjee, the first Indian Chief Justice of Lahore High Court, was a well-known philanthropist who had established several schools, colleges, hospitals and women's homes in northern India. His views on Hinduism were similar to those held by Ramkrishna. He was also a social reformer and a believer in Sanatan Dharam.

In 1944, the same year Ila was born, Sir P.C. Chatterjee's granddaughter, Asha Devi, was thirty years old. She was educated, came from a well-known family and was religious. Ramkrishna heard about her and wanted to meet her as a potential wife. He was impressed by her knowledge of the shastras and the fact that she had read the Geeta.

Ramkrishna married Asha Devi in 1944. She was curious about her husband's work with political leaders. Ramkrishna, pleased by her interest, was happy to share his thoughts about them. Asha Devi learned that Ramkrishna respected Rajendra Prasad for his learning and his gentle, humble nature, and admired Sardar Patel for his diplomatic approach to solving the country's diverse problems.

Asha Devi enjoyed spending hours in Ramkrishna's company, listening as he explained his vision for an independent India. He believed that India would become a great sovereign nation under the guidance of leaders like Rajendra Prasad and Sardar Patel. Asha Devi realized that her husband was a passionate nationalist and cared deeply for the poor and underprivileged. Out of curiosity, she asked him why he did not build charitable institutions to help the needy. Ramkrishna, in his characteristic manner, explained that charity should be silent and not ostentatious. He believed that building industries was the best form of charity, as industries would provide employment to the starving millions of the country.

In 1945, both Asha Devi and Saraswati gave birth. Asha Devi had twins—a son and a daughter, and Saraswati a daughter.

Ramkrishna finally had a son and he had no reason to marry again. But fate had something else in store for him.

Dinesh Nandini came from a Rajasthani family and had been passionate about writing since her early teenage years. She started writing at the age of thirteen, excelling in poetry and storytelling. In 1946, Dinesh Nandini was introduced to Ramkrishna in Delhi. Ramkrishna was very interested in Dinesh Nandini's literary pursuits, asking her many searching questions about her writing. On her part, the young lady was captivated by the attention from one of India's leading industrialists. Ramkrishna's short stature, and piercing eyes added to the allure. The fact that he was fifty-one years old did not matter to Dinesh Nandini. When she went back to Rajasthan, she started a letter-correspondence with Ramkrishna. He was captivated by the letters and wanted to deepen the relationship. Though his quest for a son had been fulfilled, Ramkrishna could not help himself and wanted to marry Dinesh Nandini.

When Ramkrishna proposed to her, Dinesh Nandini set forth two conditions. First, after marrying her as his sixth wife, he was not to marry again. Second, she would be allowed to continue her studies after marriage. While it took some time for Ramkrishna to accept her first condition, he readily agreed to the second. Dinesh Nandini became the first woman in Rajasthan to earn a master's degree.

Ramkrishna honoured his promise and did not marry again.

He had six sons—two with Saraswati, three with Dinesh Nandini and one with Asha Devi. In total, he had eighteen children from his four wives.

Ramkrishna, as one of the richest men in India, had bought prime properties in Delhi for his families. Each wife was settled in a palatial bungalow in Lutyens Delhi, in areas that remain prestigious even decades later, including Sikandar Road, Akbar Road, and Motilal Nehru Road. Being deeply religious, Ramkrishna gave specific instructions during the construction of these houses—each room was to have verses from the Gita inscribed on some of its walls.

Ramkrishna preferred to keep his families separate and did not encourage interaction between them. He would spend time and live in one of the houses, depending on which wife was his favourite at the time. Not only did the wives not meet each other, but the children—some of whom went to the same schools—also did not become friends with one another. In later years, Ramkrishna was to spend most of his time with Saraswati and her children at their residence on Mansingh Road.

Ramkrishna was not miserly when it came to looking after his wives and their families. He ensured they lived a good life and did not want for anything. However, he himself led a simple life. He chose a small corner room at the Mansingh Road house for himself. The room had no furniture, only a hard cotton mattress on a flat bed covered by a white sheet. The walls were adorned with pictures of gods and goddesses. Whenever he was there, Ramkrishna would sit on the mattress for hours conducting his business.

He was fond of listening to Sanskrit shlokas and was meticulous about recording his thoughts in diaries, which were always close at hand. The few noticeable items in his simple room were notebooks, fountain pens and two clocks. Ramkrishna would consult these clocks frequently, as if determined to make use of every moment of his time.

He wore simple khadi clothes—a plain kurta and dhoti. On special occasions, he would wear the Nehru topi. Even his socks were plain cotton ones. While he did not stop any of his family members from eating spicy or fried vegetarian food, his own meals were simple. His usual meal consisted of a *bajra* roti with homemade curd. The only time he looked in a mirror was during his morning shaving routine.

Ramkrishna divided his time between three residences: Mansingh Road, where Saraswati lived with her children; Sikandra Road, where Dinesh Nandini lived with her children; and Motilal Nehru Road, where Asha Devi lived with her children. However, he spent most of his time at Mansingh Road. In the afternoon, he would visit Sikandra Road, and in the evening, he would go to Motilal Nehru Road. By 8 p.m. he would return to Mansingh Road. To travel between the houses, Ramkrishna used different cars, each with its own driver.

His mornings followed a fixed routine. By 7 a.m., he would finish reading the newspapers and then go for a walk. Upon his return, he would have a two-hour massage session, which he believed was essential for a long and healthy life. Anyone who wished to meet him during those two hours could do so in the massage room. Four telephones were placed near the massage table, and Ramkrishna would take calls during this time. If there were no visitors or calls, he would dictate letters or documents to his stenographer.

Ramkrishna was not fond of fashion. He dressed simply and was against any display of ostentation. He also insisted that his family members read only religious books. If he ever caught any of his children or wives reading what he called 'cheap novels', he would throw the books out. He was also opposed to playing cards and would dispose of them if found anywhere in the house. He wanted everyone in his family to learn Sanskrit. When he travelled, he ensured that religious photos were always around him.

His one form of exercise was his morning walk, which he never missed. During his walks, a couple of staff members would always accompany him, remaining some distanced behind. Ramkrishna maintained a brisk pace as he walked through the neighbourhood. However, he often got lost, and it was his staff who would guide him back home.

One day, when Ramkrishna was out walking, he reached Teen Murti, a distance of approximately 4 km from his house on Akbar Road. At Teen Murti, there was a traffic roundabout with many roads radiating outward. Ramkrishna looked at the roads and became confused. There were no signboards to indicate their names. He did not know which road would lead him back home. As was his habit, he looked around for his staff to ask for directions. Unfortunately, none of them were in sight.

As he stood wondering how to get back home, he saw a middle-aged woman walking some distance ahead. He briskly walked up to her.

'Behen, do you know how to get to Akbar Road from here?' he asked her after greeting her with folded hands.

'Akbar Road? Bhai sahib, I am also going that way,' the woman replied with a disarming smile. She was dressed in old clothes and did not appear well off.

'Oh! That's wonderful, behen. I will walk with you then, if you don't mind,' said Ramkrishna, who treated everyone—rich or poor—with the same respect.

'Of course not. Let's walk that way,' she said, pointing towards one of the roads.

As the two walked, they got talking. Neither knew who the other was, and neither asked for the other's name.

'So, behen, what brings you here? Who are you going to meet on Akbar Road?' Ramkrishna asked, intrigued by this woman confidently walking alone in Delhi.

'Bhai sahib, now what can I say? I have fallen on hard times. I lost my husband some time ago, and I have an unwed daughter. You know what a terrible responsibility it is to have an unmarried daughter, don't you?' The woman needed only to be asked to unburden herself. As she spoke, she kept twisting the pallu of her sari in her hands, her distress evident.

Ramkrishna nodded, waiting for her to continue.

'I have heard of the great Seth Ramkrishna. I am told he lives on Akbar Road. I want to fall at his feet and beg for financial help so I can get my daughter married. After that, I can die in peace, if it comes to that,' said the woman.

Ramkrishna looked at her keenly. She was wearing a plain cotton saree, her feet were dusty from walking and her eyes were swollen, as if she had been crying.

'Oh, Seth Ramkrishna? How providential! By chance, I am also going to his house,' said Ramkrishna, smiling warmly. He wanted to help the woman in her time of need.

When they reached his house, Ramkrishna asked the woman to wait at the gate.

'I will go inside and ask Sethji for money on your behalf. By the way, how much money do you need from him?' Ramkrishna asked the woman. As one of the guards on duty walked hurriedly towards them, Ramkrishna turned slightly and gestured for the guard to go back and remain silent. He placed a finger on his lips and shook his head.

The guard understood. He knew not to question his boss. With a smile, he sauntered back to the guard house.

'Many thanks, Bhai sahib. I am so grateful to you for speaking to Sethji. I don't know how I would have asked him for money myself. He is such an important man and look at me … ' she said, gesturing to her simple sari.

'Don't worry, behen. I am sure such things don't matter to Sethji. So, how much money should I tell him you need?' Ramkrishna persisted gently.

'Bhai sahib, I wanted one thousand rupees. I know it is a large amount, but I have only one daughter, and with my husband no more, it is difficult to find a good match for her,' she said softly, her tone apologetic.

'Don't worry, behen. Let me go inside and see what can be done,' Ramkrishna reassured her.

Ramkrishna entered the house and called for his personal assistant. As he waited for him, he took a piece of paper and wrote down the amount of money to be given to the woman.

As Ramchandran, his personal assistant, hurried into the room, he handed him the slip of paper. 'Here, Ramchandran, give the woman waiting at the gate one thousand rupees,' he instructed his assistant.

Ramchandran looked at the note, then back at Ramkrishna, hesitating.

'What's the matter, Ramchandran? Go and give the money to the woman. What are you waiting for?' Ramkrishna asked, his irritation evident.

'Sethji, I am a bit confused and wanted to clarify something,' replied Ramchandran hesitantly, glancing again at the slip of paper.

'What do you want to clarify?' Ramkrishna asked sharply, thinking his assistant was questioning the act of giving.

'Sethji, you told me to give the woman one thousand rupees, but look at what you've written on this slip,' Ramchandran said, holding out the paper.

Ramkrishna took the slip impatiently, and, upon reading it, realized what had caused Ramchandran's hesitation.

'You know, Ramchandran, strange are the ways of God. I wanted to write one thousand rupees, but somehow, I added an extra zero. The amount now is indeed ten thousand rupees,' Ramkrishna said with a wry smile as he looked up, as if towards God.

'That is what I wanted to clarify, Sethji. I shall go and give the woman one thousand rupees, as you originally intended,' said Ramchandran with a huge sigh of relief.

'Not so fast, Ramchandran, not so fast,' said Ramkrishna, stopping him.

Family Life and the Quest for a Son

Ramchandran waited.

'As I said, strange are the ways of God Almighty. This is the kismet of the daughter. I knew her mother had asked for one thousand rupees, yet my hand wrote ten thousand rupees, almost on their own. So now, this is the amount you will give the woman. Let her daughter have a truly wonderful wedding,' said Ramkrishna.

Ramchandran was surprised, but was used to his boss's way of thinking and working. He retrieved ten thousand rupees from the safe, placed the slip of paper inside and put the money in a cloth *potli*.

Meanwhile, the woman was wondering if she had made a mistake in trusting the unknown man. Perhaps she should have gone inside herself to speak to Sethji.

Her thoughts were interrupted when she saw a man approaching her with a potli that seemed filled with currency notes.

'Sethji has sent this for you. Please take it,' said Ramchandran, handing her the potli.

The woman took the potli but, feeling its weight, looked at him in confusion.

'Bhai, this seems like more than one thousand rupees. Have you given me extra?' she asked.

'Maai, Sethji has sent you ten thousand rupees,' said Ramchandran with a smile, curious to see her reaction.

The woman staggered and had to steady herself using the trunk of a nearby tree.

'Ten thousand rupees?' she asked in wonder.

'Maai, the person you met on the road was Sethji himself. He wants your daughter to have a good wedding,' Ramchandran explained with great pleasure.

14

Ramkrishna's Deep Friendship with Jinnah

THE years leading up to India's independence were a busy period for Ramkrishna and the Dalmia-Jain Group. The purchase of *The Times of India* was very close to Ramkrishna's heart. He saw the newspaper both as a means to further raise his profile and as a platform to air his views to the public. His opinions were strong and sometimes extreme, but he never held back.

The Dalmia-Jain Group was among the top three industrial groups in the country. Jaidayal and Shanti Prasad were partners in the Group and managed most of the businesses under Ramkrishna's guidance. Shanti Prasad had inducted his elder brother, Shriyans Prasad Jain, into the business. Shriyans Prasad had been adopted by Ganesh Lal after the death of their father.

Ramkrishna's Deep Friendship with Jinnah

Shanti Prasad and Jaidayal were the only two male members of Ramkrishna's immediate family as, at the time, Ramkrishna had no son of his own. Thus, as the business was expanding, he readily agreed to bring Shriyans Prasad aboard as every extra male hand was welcome. Meanwhile, Jaidayal continued to be closest to his heart. Both Jaidayal and Shanti Prasad, in turn, looked up to Ramkrishna with the greatest respect and affection.

The Dalmia-Jain Group expanded its presence in the financial services sector. The ailing Bharat Insurance company, based in Lahore, was brought under the Group's control after it went into liquidation. The company had previously been owned by Lala Hari Krishan Lal, but he had been unable to manage it well, and it was placed in the hands of liquidator Khwaja Nasir Ahmed, who set a very high price for its sale. Ramkrishna wanted to own the insurance company and, in his negotiation with Nasir Ahmed, not only agreed to pay the high price but also offered an additional sum to expedite the deal.

Once he had control of Bharat Insurance, Ramkrishna entrusted its management to Shriyans Prasad, who ran it from Lahore.

Ramkrishna was active in his support of India's political leaders, and his family, too, understood that they were expected to provide assistance, both in kind and cash. Therefore, when Jayaprakash Narayan sought refuge in Lahore with Shriyans Prasad, he was provided a safe house to stay. Jayaprakash was on the run as he was being pursued by the British government for his role in the Independence movement.

However, informants tipped off the local authorities about Jayaprakash's presence in Lahore. The police came to Shriyans Prasad's house to apprehend Jayaprakash. Fortunately, some informants within the police had informed Shriyans Prasad about the impending raid. This gave the fugitive enough time to escape and leave Lahore before the police arrived. The officers searched the house but left empty-handed.

This incident was enough for the British government to expel Shriyans Prasad from Punjab. Ramkrishna relocated him to Bombay, where he managed the Dalmia-Jain Group's various businesses in western India.

The Group had expanded across the country, with businesses across the spectrum. The sugar business, their original venture, remained strong. The Group had also made a name for itself in the banking and insurance industry.

Bharat Bank, which the Group took over in 1943, had quickly expanded to 292 branches and offices throughout the country. These were running successfully, providing valuable and efficient services to local markets and industries. Shanti Prasad served as the bank's managing director.

Another bank under the Group's control was Hooghly Bank, a local institution with several branches across Calcutta. Primarily catering to small depositors, its motto was to serve the common man. Ramkrishna wanted a branch at every street corner of Calcutta. Jaidayal was the bank's chairman.

The Group also owned the Universal Bank of India, a small institution that provided banking and insurance services to Rohtas Industries and its employees.

Over the years, the Group's mills and factories had expanded significantly. Its sugar mills included the South Behar Sugar Mills, S.K.G. Sugar Limited, the Raza Sugar Company Limited and the Buland Sugar Company Limited. Other ventures included Delhi Flour Mills and the Jute and Ground Wood Mill, as well as cotton mills in western India.

The Dalmia-Jain Group had a presence in the aviation sector as well. Indian National Airways was established to link upcountry stations with the main Empire trunk air route. It operated a large fleet, including Dakotas, Vickers Vikings, Bristol Wayfarers and De Havilland Doves. Its key routes included Delhi – Lucknow – Kanpur – Allahabad – Calcutta; Delhi – Jodhpur – Karachi; Lahore – Quetta – Karachi; and Delhi – Lahore – Rawalpindi – Peshawar.

In addition to Indian National Airways, the Group also operated Dalmia-Jain Airways Limited, which specialized in the sale of vehicles and air transport. Within a short time, it became the largest company in its sector.

Beyond banking and aviation, the Group had diversified into a wide range of industries, including chemical factories, distilleries, the motor industry, cement factories, power generation, a pipe and pole factory, a vegetable ghee factory, a biscuit factory, a soap factory, a plywood factory, a playing cards and box factory, a paper mill, collieries and an asbestos factory.

Among these diverse businesses and factories, a few were especially close to Ramkrishna's heart. These included Bharat Insurance, Bharat Fire and General Insurance, and *The Times of India*. The insurance companies were among the premier firms in their sector, but the jewel in Ramkrishna's crown was *The Times of India*.

By this time, *The Times of India* had grown into India's best-known newspaper. Ramkrishna personally controlled its editorial policy. He saw the newspaper as a platform to promote and publicize his views on politics, society and religion. His opinions were strong, and despite many well-wishers advising him to tone down his rhetoric, Ramkrishna blazed forth.

Some well-wishers also cautioned Ramkrishna about his friendship with Jinnah. Ramkrishna and Jinnah were very close friends.

Ramkrishna had been a strong supporter of the Congress party and its leaders since the early 1930s. However, after the Second World War, when the provincial government took charge in India, Ramkrishna found himself disagreeing with Nehru's socialist policies. Never one to mince his words, he made it known that he disapproved of Nehru's vision for the country. Using the editorial pages of *The Times of India*, Ramkrishna published his strong views and sharp criticism of Nehru's policies.

Although the third-largest industrialist in India, behind only the Tatas and the Birlas, Ramkrishna's proximity to Jinnah made many people wary of him. This did not bother Ramkrishna in the least. The odd couple met often, addressing each other simply as 'Dalmia' and 'Jinnah' and using the more familiar *tu* and *tum* when speaking in Hindi.

Though they were neighbours in Lutyens Delhi, their friendship had begun long before. Jinnah was seventeen years older than Ramkrishna. The bond that developed between them was an unlikely friendship between polar opposites. What united them, however, was their deep love for their motherland and a shared disdain for Nehru.

Ramkrishna and Jinnah were as different as anyone could be. Jinnah was born in Karachi to a wealthy Khoja Muslim textile merchant, while Ramkrishna was a Vaishnav Bania, born into a family that had once been rich. Jinnah hated his studies, particularly mathematics, whereas mathematics and numbers were hardwired into Ramkrishna's brain. Jinnah, disinterested in school, was sent to London to study law and later earned a barrister's degree, while Ramkrishna longed to study but could not and remained without a formal education. Ramkrishna spent his time striving to build a life and livelihood, moving from Chirawa to Calcutta in search of work, while Jinnah spent his time honing his acting skills with local theatre groups that staged Shakespearean plays.

One thing they had in common was that both had married young. Jinnah wed at fifteen, just before leaving for London, but his young bride died soon after. Similarly, Ramkrishna was married at eleven, and his first wife, Narbada, passed away not long after their wedding.

Their lifestyles further underscored their differences. Jinnah was an avid meat-eater. He lived in a colonial home, where each lavish meal included fine port wines and beef. He had a taste for the finer things in life, and enjoyed smoking expensive Cuban cigars, drinking Bordeaux wines and dressing in Italian suits. In contrast, Ramkrishna was a devout Hindu who abhorred the killing of animals for food. Deeply religious, he worshipped Goddess Durga, lived according to Vedic principles, wore only khadi and practised simple living.

Even their approaches to marriage were in stark contrast. Jinnah was a monogamist even though he had religious sanction for multiple marriages. After the death of his first wife, he later married Ratti Bai, with whom he had one daughter, Dina. Ramkrishna, on the other hand, was a polygamist. After Narbada's passing, he married five more women in his relentless pursuit of a son. His quest was ultimately fulfilled—he had eighteen children from four of his wives, including six sons.

Jinnah and Ramkrishna met frequently, and their friendship deepened during the 1930s. By the latter part of the decade,

Ramkrishna had entrusted the day-to-day management of his business interests to his family, allowing him to devote more time to what he saw as serving the nation. While he continued to support the Congress, he also engaged in political discussions with Jinnah. In a sense, both men were deeply committed to India's independence, even though they followed different political parties—Jinnah was part of the Muslim League and Ramkrishna aligned with the Congress.

When talks about the possible partition of India began gaining ground, Ramkrishna discussed the issue with his friend. With the well being of the Indian nation in mind, Ramkrishna wanted an amicable settlement between the Congress and the Muslim League. Jinnah often visited Ramkrishna at his Mansingh Road residence, and the two men would sit in the drawing room and talk till the lights came on.

'Jinnah, you know that Hindus think that you are a demon retarding the progress of the country,' said Ramkrishna one evening as they sat in the drawing room. The servants had served tea and stepped away, remaining just one loud call away should Ramkrishna need anything.

'Ah! Dalmia, is that so?' Jinnah sat up with interest, as he leaned forward reaching for his cup of tea.

'Yes, yes, Jinnah. You should hear how some Hindus talk about you,' Ramkrishna chuckled.

'Ha! Not so! Ask the Muslims what I am doing for them,' Jinnah waved his hands as if waving away the statement made by his friend. Ramkrishna flinched, as if afraid that the hot tea would spill on him.

'But why divide Hindus and Muslims like this, Jinnah? What will it achieve?' Ramkrishna turned serious. He was genuinely concerned—and also relieved that no tea had been spilled.

'I could rejoin the Congress,' Jinnah mused, the hint of a question in his voice as he looked speculatively at Ramkrishna.

'Then why don't you?' This time it was Ramkrishna who leaned forward in anticipation.

'You know, Dalmia, don't you, that I want to be a leader in the Congress too,' Jinnah said languidly.

'Of course, of course. You will be a leader. But perhaps not the top leader, as you are today in the Muslim League,' Ramkrishna was quick to tell his friend enthusiastically.

'Look, that is the reason why I don't want to rejoin the Congress,' explained Jinnah. He wanted to lead the Congress, but knew that was not possible.

'Oh, Jinnah! You are ambitious to becoming the Caliph of Turkey in an independent Pakistan!' exclaimed Ramkrishna in mild frustration as he looked at his friend in fond exasperation.

Jinnah smiled at his friend's analogy.

'Look Dalmia, at least give me credit for bringing together the Jee Huzurs and Nawabs who once served the British and making them serve the country instead,' said Jinnah, waving a finger under Ramkrishna's nose.

The matter rested there as the two friends, in unspoken mutual consent, focused on their tea and water and talked of matters other than politics.

Ramkrishna was drawn to Jinnah as he believed his friend to be a man of towering vanity yet of unassailable personal honesty. Because of this, Ramkrishna was convinced that Jinnah was incorruptible. Jinnah was also a man of few words.

'I do not make statements frequently and reply only at the appropriate time,' remarked Jinnah one evening as the two men spent time together.

'Maybe that is why your speeches have such a profound impact,' Ramkrishna concurred.

Ramkrishna's faith in Jinnah's character was strengthened by the incidents he witnessed and the stories he heard.

On one occasion, the son of a prominent Muslim League leader—a close friend of Jinnah's—approached him for a character certificate. The young man requested Jinnah to certify that he knew him personally. Jinnah had no qualms about doing so as he did indeed know the son well.

As he took out a sheet of paper and a pen to write out the certificate, he asked the son why he needed it. The son explained that it was required for his appointment to the Finance Committee in the Legislative Assembly.

The moment Jinnah heard this, he stopped. He looked at the paper and then tore it up.

'I will not be able to give you such a certificate,' he said, firmly screwing the cap of his pen back on.

'But why? You know me, don't you, sir?' the young man asked, puzzled.

'Yes, I do. But if you were on the Finance Committee, I might feel embarrassed to oppose your arguments in the Assembly,' explained Jinnah.

Though the young man and his father were unhappy, Jinnah stood firm in his convictions.

Despite their ideological differences, the two men found enough common ground to maintain their relationship. Each tried to persuade the other to embrace his own ideology, but even when these attempts failed, their relationship remained intact.

One evening, Jinnah was at Ramkrishna's residence. As he sipped his tea, he mentioned that he would be leaving Delhi for a few days.

The two men were sitting in the open veranda, enjoying the mild weather. The staff had served them their choice of beverages and some light snacks. The birds were returning to their perches in the trees and the evening was filled with their light twittering.

'Where are you going this time, Jinnah?' Ramkrishna asked with interest.

'I am going to Karachi. The people there have invited me to address a rally,' said Jinnah as he took a bite of the savoury snack before him. He liked it and quickly took another bite.

'That is interesting. What will you say?' asked Ramkrishna curiously. He, too, took a bite of the snack as he saw Jinnah enjoying it.

'Dalmia, why don't you come with me and hear for yourself?' Jinnah suggested. He looked at Ramkrishna watchfully and waited for his answer.

'Oh yes, I would like that. But you must agree to let me speak freely at your rally,' Ramkrishna replied almost immediately, an impish gleam in his eyes.

Jinnah looked keenly at Ramkrishna for a moment before breaking into laughter.

'You will ruin all my plans, Dalmia. Best if you stay here,' he said, still chuckling, as he leaned forward and patted Ramkrishna on the thigh.

'But I have a cement factory in Karachi. I could visit it as well,' Ramkrishna pressed the matter, knowing full well he wouldn't actually go, but enjoying the opportunity to pull Jinnah's leg.

'No, no, you are best here,' said Jinnah. He looked at his friend and smiled fondly to signal that was the end of the matter.

While relations between Jinnah and Dalmia remained cordial, the same could not be said for Jinnah's interactions with other Congress leaders. Jinnah and Gandhi did not see eye to eye on many matters.

Ramkrishna often tried to change Jinnah's perception of Gandhi, but did not make any headway.

'Why do you refuse to change your opinion about Gandhi?' he asked Jinnah one day after a long argument about the Congress and its leaders.

'I have told you my misgivings many times, Dalmia. But you don't seem to understand. Fine, let me tell you a story—maybe then you will see my point,' Jinnah told his friend, irritated by Ramkrishna's relentless efforts to persuade him to negotiate with the Congress.

'Go on, Jinnah. I am eager to hear,' said Ramkrishna, sitting up in anticipation.

'Do you remember when Gandhi returned to India after attending the Round Table Conference in London?' Jinnah started telling his story. As he spoke he looked at the distant tree rather than at Ramkrishna.

'Yes, I remember,' Ramkrishna nodded.

'I wanted to meet him and sought to set up a meeting. But do you know what happened? He refused to meet me,' said Jinnah softly, still staring into the distance as if replaying the moment in his mind.

'He refused? Really? Do you know why?' asked Ramkrishna, mystified.

'From what I was told, Gandhi said he was praying for light but saw none. He said this in reference to me. Now, do you not think that was uncalled for?' Jinnah's voice was sharp as he finally looked his friend straight in the eye.

Ramkrishna could not help but agree. However, he had another point to make.

'You always refer to the Mahatma as Gandhi. And you are constantly criticizing him in public. Do you think that is fine?' asked Ramkrishna, switching tracks.

Jinnah merely shrugged.

'Listen, a great person will always remain great. If one spits at the moon, it will only fall back on one's own face,' persisted Ramkrishna.

Jinnah remained quiet and returned his gaze to the distant tree.

After a while, he finally looked at Ramkrishna. It seemed he had made up his mind to speak.

'You know Malviyaji?' Jinnah asked him.

'Of course I know him,' replied Ramkrishna, surprised that Jinnah even needed to ask.

'But do you also know that every time I visit Malviyaji at his house, he has the carpet I walked on washed and disinfected? Not just that, he also ensures the plates I used and the tablecloth I touched are thoroughly cleaned. I have expressed my resentment to him, but what does he do? Nothing,' Jinnah said, spreading his hands in frustration.

He looked at Ramkrishna, and there was hurt in his eyes.

This time it was Ramkrishna who remained silent.

With his close ties to Congress leaders, Ramkrishna tried many times to broker peace between Jinnah and the Congress. His efforts intensified when it became apparent that Jinnah was adamant on the division of the country along religious lines. He had numerous conversations with Jinnah about the need for Partition. He even approached Sardar Patel, offering to use his influence to persuade Jinnah to abandon his obstinate demand for carving out Pakistan from India. Patel, however, did not take Ramkrishna seriously; he not only discouraged him, but outright dismissed the idea of him parleying with Jinnah on the matter.

Ramkrishna's friendship with Jinnah led many Hindus to believe that he was anti-Hindu. Some even called him a traitor to the cause. Ramkrishna ignored such criticism as he believed in Jinnah as a Person. He continued urging Jinnah to give up the idea of Partition. Jinnah, in turn, agreed to meet a senior Congress leader at Ramkrishna's residence to discuss the issue. He was open to a settlement based on full autonomy for the provinces, with only three subjects—defence, communications and foreign affairs—remaining under central control.

During a lengthy discussion with Rajendra Prasad at his residence, Ramkrishna requested him to consult with Nehru and Patel. He still wanted to help bring about an amicable solution to the problem. However, news about his talks with Prasad leaked. That night, a broadcast on London Radio reported that a merchant was attempting to broker an amicable settlement between the Congress and the Muslim League.

The following day, Indian newspapers carried reports quoting a Congress spokesman who dismissed the significance of Ramkrishna's negotiations, saying that he was, after all, just a merchant. Jinnah, too, had heard the radio and read the morning newspapers. He immediately telephoned Ramkrishna.

'Look at the mentality of your own people, Dalmia. Now, I will not agree to anything less than an independent sovereign state of Pakistan,' Jinnah thundered over the phone.

Despite this, Jinnah told Ramkrishna of his willingness to implement a population exchange between India and Pakistan. He believed it would be best for all Hindus to leave Pakistan and for all Muslims in India to migrate to Pakistan. Undeterred by the earlier rejection of his mediation, Ramkrishna once again approached Patel and other senior Congress leaders. He told them of Jinnah's proposal. However, this idea, too, was not acceptable to the Congress leaders. They said that the Hindus of Pakistan and Muslims of India were their kith and kin and that they were prepared to sacrifice their own lives to protect them.

However, the promises were written on water. Partition took place, and people on both sides were brutally killed. The Hindus in Pakistan were either compelled to convert to Islam or left to live in constant fear and misery.

15

Division of the Dalmia-Jain Group

FOLLOWING Independence, Ramkrishna was deeply disillusioned with the policies followed by India's new government, especially those of Prime Minister Nehru. He used his newspapers to air his grievances openly. In addition, he spoke with his friends and associates about what he believed the government was doing wrong.

His residence became the gathering place for these discussions. Many an evening was spent in the drawing room, where Ramkrishna passionately expounded on his views to those gathered.

'Look at us, just look at us,' he said, throwing his arms wide as if to encompass the entire country.

'We have debts amounting to several thousand crores of rupees. And yet, look at Europe—even a small country like

Division of the Dalmia-Jain Group

Luxembourg, let alone bigger countries like Germany, is making progress after the World War. Forget Europe, even Japan, here in Asia, is trying to rebuild after the war.'

'So why do you think this is happening, Sethji?' asked an associate sitting a little away from Ramkrishna.

'It is simple. For the success of a nation, its head and his lieutenants must be fearless, powerful and capable of adapting policies to changing circumstances. It does not matter whether the country is aligned or non-aligned. Look at the USA and the USSR—they are politically opposed, yet both are progressing fast,' Ramkrishna said, raising his voice so even those sitting farther away could hear.

The group nodded, waiting for him to continue.

'Had we declared India a Hindu state in 1947, I am telling you, other communities—the Parsis, Muslims and others—would have received every protection. We all would have been happy, like the small and large nations of Europe,' said Ramkrishna with conviction.

'But Sethji, doesn't the Prime Minister also want our country to industrialize?' asked another person in the group.

'Of course, no doubt India is making substantial progress in industrialization and scientific technology. But look around you—poverty and rising prices are rampant. Also, you know that the retirement age for government servants varies from state to state. In the USA, there is no fixed retirement age for important government posts. It is tragic that although one gains valuable experience and maturity of thought after the age of fifty, in India, we retire government officials just as they reach the peak of their capabilities, self-confidence and decision-making skills,' Ramkrishna said passionately.

He looked around to see if those present were absorbing all that he was saying. When he saw that they were listening intently, he continued.

'My father was a very wise man. He used to tell me that there is no doubt that a man of fifty-five, with years of experience, becomes wise. Even an unwise person, given enough experience, can gain wisdom—just as the hard stone at the top of a well gradually wears down from the constant friction of a soft rope drawing water,' Ramkrishna told the group who was listening to him with interest. Some in the group kept nodding their heads as if they agreed.

Ramkrishna's views were evident to everyone as they were aired through *The Times of India*. Even his opinions expressed in private gatherings reached the ears of the ruling leaders.

Shanti Prasad and Jaidayal repeatedly cautioned Ramkrishna to tone down his views.

'Pitaji, you know that we industrialists need the support of the ruling government. Your tirade against the government, especially Nehru, is not conducive to our businesses,' said Shanti Prasad one day at the Mansingh Road house in Delhi.

Jaidayal also tried to reason with his elder brother.

'Bhaiji, we are all upset about the government's handling of Partition. But do you have to criticize the government's failure to take appropriate and swift action for the rehabilitation of refugees from Pakistan? And your strong stance on cow slaughter—must you keep blaming the government for not doing enough about it?' Jaidayal was more forceful in his argument than Shanti Prasad.

Ramkrishna was bewildered by their admonitions.

'So, you believe I should keep quiet and not speak my mind?' he asked, looking from one to the other. Neither met his eyes.

'No, no, we are not saying that ... ' both rushed to refute the charge.

'Then what are you saying?' Ramkrishna was perplexed. He could not understand why Shanti Prasad and Jaidayal were advising him to hold back.

'We are just saying that all the noise surrounding you and your proclamations is affecting our businesses,' Jaidayal finally explained.

Now Ramkrishna became agitated.

'Business? You're talking about business? Do you even know what Nehru has said about me? When I criticized his socialist tilt towards the communist block, he said, "Dalmia is an ugly man with an ugly face and an ugly mind and an ugly heart. Just because he owns a few newspapers, he claims to be an expert of foreign affairs?" He called me ugly!'

Ramkrishna was furious. The barb about his looks had hit home.

The other two men looked at him silently.

'Even after this, you want me to keep quiet? Eh? The man does not remember all the money I have given him and his newspaper—*National Herald*,' continued Ramkrishna, his voice rising in an anger. Agitated, he got up and began pacing the room.

When all their gentle and not-so-gentle counsel failed to have any effect on Ramkrishna, Shanti Prasad and Jaidayal realized they would have to work out another way to resolve the problem. His public criticism of the government was just one of the issues they wished to raise with him. Simmering beneath the surface were other issues that were of concern to both Jaidayal and Shanti Prasad.

One matter that bothered them was the fact that Ramkrishna now had four wives. Three of them were much younger than Ramkrishna and were bearing children in quick succession. By this time, Ramkrishna already had four children, including a son.

Both men were aware of Ramkrishna's obsession with having sons. With three wives still capable of bearing children, they could not be certain how many sons he might ultimately have. Until his first son was born, Jaidayal and Shanti Prasad had been the only male inheritors of the business.

For Shanti Prasad, the matter was even more serious. When he had married Rama, she had been Ramkrishna's only child. From an inheritance perspective, Shanti Prasad had assumed that Ramkrishna's share of the business would come to Rama and himself, giving them a clear 50 per cent ownership, with Jaidayal inheriting the other half. However, a decade after their marriage, his father-in-law had married again in quick succession, changing the situation. Ironically, Shanti Prasad and Rama's children were in fact older than Rama's siblings!

Both Jaidayal and Shanti Prasad knew that Ramkrishna loved them more than life itself. Yet, they could not be certain how the businesses would be handled after him. They assumed that, eventually, the businesses would be divided equally among all the male heirs, leaving them with only a small fraction of what they had all created together. The two men wanted to secure their own positions in the business, especially as they believed that a large part of its expansion and success was due to their efforts.

Another matter that troubled Jaidayal and Shanti Prasad also revolved around Ramkrishna's new wives. Ever since his last two marriages, the two men had been facing an unusual problem. Male relatives, especially brothers, of the new wives had begun voicing their desire to be part of the Dalmia-Jain Group. Their desire stemmed from the fact that there were no other male family members in the business apart from Jaidayal and Shanti Prasad. The wives too believed that that if a son-in-law and his brother could be inducted into the business and made partners, then their brothers too had just as much right to be included.

Shanti Prasad and Jaidayal did not like this interference by 'outsiders' in their business affairs.

Both men were business managers, while finances and risk were managed by Ramkrishna. A speculator at heart, Ramkrishna was always willing to take even uncalculated risks. He believed that the only way to grow faster was to take risks, even if some ventures failed spectacularly. Jaidayal and Shanti Prasad, however, believed that while it was fine to take risks in the satta bazaar, when it came to brick-and-mortar businesses, risk had to be managed. They knew that as long as Ramkrishna was in charge, they would have no say in these matters. They wanted to consolidate the businesses rather than take unnecessary risks.

Jaidayal and Shanti Prasad decided to have a discussion and request Ramkrishna to divide the businesses among the three of them. They agreed that this was the only way to protect the businesses and shield a large part of the empire from the wrath of the government, which could be unleashed at any time due to Ramkrishna's refusal to be silenced. They also agreed that if they each had their own share of the business, the male relatives of Ramkrishna's wives could not legitimately or morally claim a share in it. The matter of inheritance would also be addressed.

'I think this would be best for the businesses. After all, we have hundreds of workers. If something happens to our business, it won't just affect us, but all of them as well,' Jaidayal said to Ramkrishna.

The three men were sitting in the drawing room. It was evening, and the light had mellowed. The lamps had been lit, but parts of the room remained in shadow. The staff had retreated, sensing that an important discussion was about to take place. Both younger men had serious expressions.

'Pitaji, you decide how the businesses should be divided. We will accept whatever you say,' Shanti Prasad added.

Ramkrishna was completely unprepared for this. He felt a sense of betrayal. For a while, he was speechless, looking silently from one to the other. Jaidayal and Shanti Prasad, too, were uncomfortable. They hung their heads, avoiding his gaze.

Ramkrishna saw their discomfort, but their body language made it clear that the two men were dead serious in their demand. He did not like the proposal, but he also saw that the two people he held dearest were united in this. He loved Jaidayal more than anyone else in his life, and Shanti Prasad was like a son to him. Ramkrishna was perceptive enough to realize that the two younger men were determined to see the division of the business through.

It was also evident that Jaidayal and Shanti Prasad had spent considerable time discussing the potential split before coming to him. The die had been cast, and there was no going back on the decision already made by his two trusted partners.

Ramkrishna was nothing if not pragmatic. If the business had to be split, he decided, it was best done amicably and without any public spectacle. He did not want the world to laugh at his family, nor did he want tongues wagging and gossip

Division of the Dalmia-Jain Group

spreading. Though fearless in most aspects of life, he deeply valued respect in the world and from it. He told Jaidayal and Shanti Prasad that he was willing to divide the businesses but needed a little time to work out the details.

In May 1948, they met at the Jain family home in Mussoorie. Ramkrishna stated that he wanted to retain control of Bharat Bank, Bharat Insurance, the Times of India Group and a few smaller businesses. He told the two younger men that they could divide the remaining businesses between themselves.

Without any legal paperwork or public announcement, the Dalmia-Jain Group split quietly and without controversy.

Shanti Prasad took control of Dalmianagar (Rohtas Industries, Rohtas Quarries and Dehri-Rohtas Light Railway), Bharat Bank, the three jute mills (Albion, Lothian and New Central), Bharat and Maheshpur collieries, Govan Brothers (along with its eight subsidiary companies), National Safe Deposit and Cold Storage, and the Allahabad Law Journal Company.

Jaidayal received Dalmia Cement, Orissa Cement (a new company that was to commission a 500-tonne-per-day plant at Rajgangpur in 1951), Kharkhari Coal Company, S.K.G. Sugar Ltd, Patiala Biscuit Manufacturers, Lesco Chemical Works, Bharat Fire and General Insurance, and the relatively minor Universal Bank of India.

Ramkrishna retained Bennett, Coleman & Co and other publications (*Bharat Journals* and the *Civil and Military Gazette*); the two textile mills (SSB and MDM); Allen Berry and Dalmia-Jain Airways; Bharat Insurance, Punjab National Bank and Gwalior Bank; Lahore Electric Supply Company; Dalmia Dadri Cement and Jaipur Udyog; and the group's trading and investment arms—Dalmia Cement and Paper Marketing and Dalmia Investment Company.

A few years later, some minor business exchanges took place—Govan Brothers ended up with Jaidayal, Patiala Biscuit went to Ramkrishna and S.K.G. Sugar was transferred to Shanti Prasad.

Despite being the third-largest business group in the country, the split occurred without any noise in the media, and the public remained largely unaware. Though relations between the three men suffered for a short time, they were soon repaired and cordiality was maintained between them and their families. However, for Ramkrishna, the separation felt like losing half of his energy and strength, as Jaidayal and Shanti Prasad—his 'left and right hands'—were no longer by his side in business.

16

Ramkrishna Is Sent to Jail

RAMKRISHNA was busy managing the Times of India Group, using the full power of the newspaper to air his views about the Congress.

He felt a deep sense of betrayal by the Congress. Throughout the pre-Independence years, he had supported the Congress through generous financial contributions—not only to the party but also to individual Congress leaders, including a monthly allowance of Rs 500 to Nehru. He had believed that in recognition of his long-standing contributions, the Congress leadership would consider at least some of his firm beliefs—especially those concerning the prevention of cow slaughter, the promotion of Sanatan Dharma and welfare work for the refugees of Partition. However, post-Independence, he found himself disillusioned.

It is possible that the Congress might have been more sympathetic to some of his views had he not been so outspoken in his criticism of Nehru. Hardly a day passed without *The Times of India* publishing a scathing article attacking the government.

The country had been pushed into a blood-soaked Partition, and millions of bewildered refugees had made their way to India from East Pakistan (now Bangladesh) and West Pakistan. Ramkrishna was deeply moved by their suffering and spent lakhs of rupees on their protection and welfare.

Seeking others' support for refugee rehabilitation, Ramkrishna embarked on extensive tours of Punjab, Rajasthan and Calcutta, addressing gatherings of thousands of people. In these meetings, he spoke openly and boldly, exposing what he saw as the Congress government's inaction and unsound policies.

Ramkrishna also vehemently criticized the Congress government's policy of controlling the price of jute and jute goods for export. He argued that such controls would lead to a loss in foreign exchange, estimating the loss at approximately Rs 18 crore per annum. This included the earnings of investors in the jute industry and revenue to the government in income tax. He also said that importers would earn substantial profits. Ramkrishna raised such an outcry that the question was discussed in Parliament. Subsequently, the government raised the export duty on jute manufacturers from Rs 50 to Rs 750 per tonne. Ramkrishna was proved right.

Nehru remained the primary target of Ramkrishna's ire. While Nehru seethed and simmered at Ramkrishna's criticisms, Ramkrishna continued to boldly highlight the government's lapses and shortcomings.

Ramkrishna Is Sent to Jail

To add to his controversial image, Ramkrishna was seen as a close friend of Jinnah—one of the most hated men in India. This perception was further reinforced when Jinnah sold his sprawling bungalow in Lutyens Delhi to Ramkrishna.

As Jinnah was to leave for Karachi on 7 August 1947 to assume his role as the first Governor General of Pakistan, he had to sell his residence—10 Aurangzeb Road—as it was clear he would never return. Since he was departing in a hurry and did not have much time, he sold it to his close friend, Ramkrishna, for Rs 4 lakh.

However, Ramkrishna never lived in the bungalow he bought from Jinnah. Instead, he converted it into the headquarters for the anti-cow slaughter movement—a cause very close to his heart. Every day, he would feed a cow before eating anything himself. He worshipped the cow and wanted a complete ban on cow slaughter. He wrote to Gandhi several times, requesting him to do something about it. In his letters, he described the brutal and violent ways in which cows were killed. However, Gandhi did not support Ramkrishna. Unperturbed by the lack of response, Ramkrishna did what he did best—he ran editorials in his newspapers, including one in which he advocated for a cow economy as a solution to inflation.

Thus, even before the ink had dried on the sale deed, Ramkrishna hoisted a green flag over Jinnah's former residence—symbolizing his vociferous demand for a nationwide ban on cow slaughter. It was indeed ironic that Jinnah's home became the centre for the protest against cow slaughter.

The government was displeased with Ramkrishna acquiring Jinnah's house, as the bungalow was a symbol of the man responsible for the Partition of the country. Nehru wanted the government to requisition the property and intended to allocate it to Rajkumari Amrit Kaur, an Indian activist and politician. However, Ramkrishna would have none of it—if he could not keep the house, then the government would not have it either. He sold the bungalow to the Dutch Government, and Jinnah's house became the property of a foreign nation.

For obvious reasons, this further antagonized the government, intensifying the undercurrents between Ramkrishna and the administration. Ramkrishna, on his part, continued his tirades against Nehru through both *The Times of India* and the public gatherings he addressed. The government, on its part, was looking for a way to silence Ramkrishna.

The opportunity presented itself to Nehru five years after Independence.

Astrologers had played a significant role in Ramkrishna's life. He believed in them and often followed their advice blindly. In his early years, an astrologer had predicted that he would gain wealth, and he did—even though the astrologer himself had lost out on the deal.

Ramkrishna's misfortunes, however, began with the advice of an astrologer. Haveli Ram, who had Ramkrishna's ear in the 1940s, warned him after Independence that a financial crisis was imminent in India and that the prevailing chaos would only intensify. He advised Ramkrishna to curtail his businesses.

Ramkrishna, who had blind faith in the astrologer, decided to hive off his businesses. He sold his drum factory in Bombay for a mere Rs 12 lakh and disposed of two cotton mills, woollen mills and several small businesses at throwaway prices.

His troubles did not end there. In 1955, during his maiden speech in Parliament, Feroze Gandhi, a member of parliament and also the son-in-law of Nehru, accused Ramkrishna of embezzling Rs 2.20 crore from Bharat Insurance. Though Ramkrishna vehemently denied the allegations, Nehru saw this as an opportunity to silence his vocal critic. He ordered an inquiry into the 'scam'. Annadhanam, a chartered accountant, was appointed investigator. The matter went to court.

Sir Dingle Foot, a British barrister, served as Ramkrishna's counsel. The main matter before the court was the alleged conspiracy to divert funds from Bharat Insurance Company to recoup Ramkrishna's losses in share speculation.

Ramkrishna was the chairman of the Board of Directors and the principal officer of Bharat Insurance Company, while G.L. Chokhani acted as the company's agent in Bombay. Chokhani regularly bought and sold securities on behalf of the company, but there was no board resolution authorizing him to do so. It was alleged that these transactions were carried out by Chokhani under the instructions of Ramkrishna. Both Ramkrishna and Chokhani maintained that it was indeed true that Ramkrishna had given Chokhani general authority to buy and sell securities.

Due to this general trust between them, Chokhani was in the habit of conducting transactions independently, without instructions from Ramkrishna. Between 1954 and 1955, these transactions resulted in massive losses, amounting to over Rs 2.20 crore. It was alleged that, to cover these losses, Chokhani diverted funds from Bharat Insurance. Further, to conceal the unauthorized transfer of money, funds were transferred from one company to another, and the accounts of the insurance company were falsified—ultimately leading to losses for policyholders.

Ramkrishna maintained that he had no involvement with the day-to-day workings of the company. He stated that after authorizing Chokhani in 1953 to buy and sell securities, the latter did so on his own thereafter. He claimed that he was unaware of Chokhani's modus operandi, which ultimately led to the diversion of funds. While he admitted that Chokhani had informed him about the losses incurred, he insisted that Chokhani had also assured him that he would arrange for funds to cover them. He categorically denied that he was a party to Chokhani's actions.

Chokhani, on his part, admitted to diverting funds to cover the losses. He, too, asserted that Ramkrishna was not involved in the day-to-day operations of the trades and financial dealings. Chokhani explained that he had executed the transactions because he expected that the broking company would eventually recover the losses, at which point the money would be returned to Bharat Insurance. He maintained that he considered the transactions as a form of lending by the insurance company to the broker and saw nothing wrong with it. He emphatically maintained that had he known his actions were illegal, he would not have done it. He would, instead, have sought other means to raise the money required. Given his strong creditworthiness in Bombay's business circles, he would have raised a loan through his network.

The courts, however, found both Ramkrishna and Chokhani guilty, and sentenced them to two years of imprisonment in Tihar Jail.

Nehru had accomplished two objectives with the inquiry that led to Ramkrishna's jail sentence. First, the inquiry itself ensured that his most vocal critic quietened down. Nehru believed that Ramkrishna would find it difficult to be as strident in his criticism once the charges of corruption were in court. For the time being, Nehru had secured peace in the media.

The second result of the jail sentence after the inquiry was a more far-reaching one. At the time of his inquiry and conviction, Ramkrishna was India's third-largest industrialist, renowned not just in India but across the world. The entire business community in India knew of Ramkrishna's association with the Congress, as well as the generous financial contributions he had made since the early 1920s—both to the party and to its leaders. His conviction sent shockwaves through industrial and business circles, creating an atmosphere of fear.

The refrain, whispered in hushed tones and in private, was that if this could happen to the third-largest industrialist in India, who had supported the party and its leaders for decades, it could happen to any one of them. Business owners became cautious, avoiding any public expression of their political views.

The Licence Raj had already been unleashed by the government. With Ramkrishna's jail sentence, business owners understood that if they wanted to continue their enterprises, they had to remain on the right side of the government—both in reality and in appearance. This practice of aligning with whichever government is in power continues till today.

Ramkrishna, meanwhile, was determined to repay the funds to the company to ensure that the policyholders would not suffer. He believed that once he returned the money, he could escape his jail term. His well-wishers advised him to first negotiate with the government and secure an assurance that his sentence would be revoked before submitting the money to the court. For all his street-smart instincts, Ramkrishna was naïve and trusting in many matters. He believed that if he repaid the money, the very basis for his conviction would cease to exist and the government would act logically and fairly. So, he set out to raise the necessary funds.

However, he had no liquid assets, having sold off most of his businesses on the advice of the astrologer. The one major business he still owned was the Times of India Group. He also had some shares in Sawai Madhopur Cement. Both these businesses were money spinners. Ramkrishna was reluctant to let go of the Times of India Group as he passionately believed that running the newspaper was his true calling, but he needed the money.

The very businessmen and industrialists who had envied his ownership of *The Times of India* and had wished that they could own it now hesitated even to explore the possibility of buying the media enterprise. No one was ready to lend money to Ramkrishna against the security of his businesses, all of which were profit-making. Ramkrishna's conviction had unsettled them. No one wanted to be at the receiving end of Nehru's vengeful wrath. Time was running out for Ramkrishna.

With no buyers for his business and no lenders, Ramkrishna asked Shanti Prasad to lend him the money, offering the Times of India Group as security and proposing to sell his stake in the cement company as well. However, Shanti Prasad wanted to purchase the businesses outright. He claimed he did not have the funds to pay the fair market value of the businesses but was ready to give his father-in-law just enough to cover the repayment to Bharat Insurance and refill the policyholders' accounts. The understanding between the two men was that once Ramkrishna was out of jail and had the means to repay

Shanti Prasad, the Times of India Group would be sold back to him.

With no other choice, Ramkrishna agreed. Without any formal paperwork or legal agreement, the ownership of his flagship company changed hands. Shanti Prasad, after he gained the ownership of the company, increased the share capital from Rs 60 lakh to Rs 2 crore by the addition of preference and equity shares. Thus, when the time came for Ramkrishna to explore the possibility of buying back his much-loved company, he found that he could not afford it.

Ramkrishna never truly recovered from the loss. However, he found solace in the fact that the ownership of *The Times of India* remained within his family. It would have been unbearable for him had an outsider taken control of the newspaper.

Ramkrishna's well-wishers were proven right. Even after he had repaid the money in full and requested a revocation of his jail term, the government insisted in court that the sentence be implemented in full.

He was sent to Tihar Jail in Delhi. His family was grief-stricken. His children faced ridicule and harassment in school. Newspaper headlines across India and around the world screamed the news of the conviction and imprisonment of the third richest man in India. Every wife and every child of Ramkrishna was shaken.

Ramkrishna, however, took the court's decision on his chin. Though he believed he had been wrongly convicted, he chose to look upon his imprisonment as a chance to atone for the sins of his past and present life. He wrote a letter to his family. Addressed to his wives and children, the letter was written in Hindi.

He wrote:

Dear ones,

Today is a very happy and opportune day for you. You will realize this after some time. As for me, my Ma Jagdamba has given me this very blessed day. Today, I am as happy as a poor man who gains an empire or an emperor blessed with a son in old age. Those who have faith in God should acknowledge that He does good for everyone. We should be grateful to Ma for inspiring the judges to grant me this happy opportunity to go to jail. Call her Ma, or God, or Rama, or Krishna or Shiva—for me, they are all one.

The Goddess has given me the chance to burn away the sins committed by me in my past or present life by going to jail. If you have true affection for me, give up your attachment to wealth, family members and even to me. Every human being is born according to their karma, but their duty is to devote their life to the good of humanity. Just as a dream is not real, this world is also a dream. Education is meaningless if you have not learnt your duty clearly.

You are a real, eternal and happy soul. You must meditate on who you are, where you have come from and where you will go. If nothing has been done so far, try to do good for all, not only in India but all over the world. If possible, write down your mistakes in a notebook and pray to the kind Ma to grant you the wisdom not to commit any mistakes in the future. Do not be forgetful about the future and adopt the path of truth.

Crores of kings and ordinary people have come and gone, leaving no trace. Their bodies have turned to dust. Happiness lies in the soul. Try to understand this. Then,

Ramkrishna Is Sent to Jail

I shall know that by adopting the right path, you have satisfied me.

My message is to emphasize that this not jail for me, but a pilgrimage.

May Ma Jagdamba bless you all.

For the first six months, Ramkrishna was in the main Central Jail of Tihar. He was housed in a room with a large compound. He was allowed to meet relatives and friends for two to three hours once a week, with a jail officer present during these meetings.

Two people were allowed to meet Ramkrishna daily. One was Pandit Sudhakar, a Sanskrit scholar. He came every day to teach Ramkrishna Sanskrit and read the Devi Bhagwat to him. The other was his personal servant, who brought him food. Since 1951, Ramkrishna had been following a strict diet, consuming only fruit, juices and milk.

Despite eating only home-prepared food, Ramkrishna fell ill in jail. Initially, the doctors kept him under observation, but his condition continued to deteriorate. On the recommendation of the medical team, he was moved to Irwin Hospital.

One of the richest men in India was placed in a common ward at the hospital, with only a partition to provide him some privacy. The corridor adjacent to his room was a thoroughfare within the hospital, used by thousands of patients, including tuberculosis patients who coughed incessantly as they passed through. Near his room was a small, open courtyard, which was used by the children of patients and their attendants to play as well as to urinate and defecate. As a result, the courtyard was infested with flies, many of which made their way into the common ward where Ramkrishna and other patients were housed.

Now that he was in the hospital, Ramkrishna was allowed more visitors. Many important and well-known people came to see him and were appalled to see the condition of his room and surrounding environment. On one occasion, Sardarni Hukam Singh, wife of the Speaker of the Lok Sabha, visited Ramkrishna. She was so overwhelmed by the foul smells and the swarms of flies that she fainted. It was Ramkrishna who had to help to revive her.

Ramkrishna spent his time not only with prominent figures but also with common people. The hospital was filled with poor patients who had come for treatment. From his room, he observed the way they were cared for. He would often speak with them, and they, in turn, were happy to converse with a 'big man'. Through these conversations, Ramkrishna realized that many of them were sent home without being given proper treatment, which often led to their deaths after they returned home. Ramkrishna was empathetic, but could do nothing as he, himself, was a prisoner.

Ramkrishna was released after two years. When he arrived home, his family and staff were waiting for him. The children had strewn flowers all along the long driveway to welcome him home. As Ramkrishna stepped out of the car and walked towards the gathering, he could feel the flower petals through the soft velvet shoes he was wearing. He looked at the flowers and then at the waiting people.

'What is this?' he asked, pointing to the scattered petals. He lifted his foot as if to check whether he was trampling them.

'Bapu, we wanted to welcome you back,' said one of his daughters, jumping from one foot to the other in excitement.

'That is fine, but why have you spoilt so many flowers for a momentary pleasure?' he chided gently as he pressed the child close in a hug.

The little girl was disheartened. She had spent a considerable amount of time picking the flowers from the garden and then strewing them carefully along the driveway. She had tears in her eyes at the mild reprimand.

Ramkrishna disliked emotional outbursts, considering them a sign of weakness. He noticed his daughter's tears, and a flicker of disapproval crossed his face. He turned to the young girl.

'Tears? What are they for, my child? I am ashamed to see a daughter of mine crying. You were Jhansi ki Rani in your past life, remember? She never cried. She fought for what was right. Learn to face life, and never show me your weak side,' said Ramkrishna as he continued walking towards the main door of the bungalow.

She nodded and wiped her tears with the sleeve of her dress.

His young daughter forgotten, Ramkrishna turned to exchange friendly words with the domestic staff. They had been waiting eagerly for their master's return. The staff respected Ramkrishna, for he had simple needs and was easy to look after.

17

Illness Takes a Toll on Ramkrishna

AFTER his release from jail, Ramkrishna spent his time managing his domestic and business affairs while immersing himself in religion and spirituality. Although he had sold off some of his businesses before his imprisonment, he still retained a few, even after losing the Times of India Group. Upon his release, he resumed overseeing the management of these profit-making ventures. While he had professionals managing the businesses, Ramkrishna remained the primary decision-maker.

Meanwhile, the government had launched more inquiries and investigations into Ramkrishna's businesses. The Tax Department also initiated probes. The Vivian Bose Commission, set up by the Government in 1956 to investigate the alleged frauds in the D-J Group, had discovered that the Group had committed numerous crimes, including criminal conspiracy, criminal breach of trust, cheating, forgery and income tax violations. Even after Ramkrishna was released from prison, the tax cases dragged on.

Ramkrishna had neither the heart nor the energy to engage in these legal battles, which he believed were part of a witch-hunt by the government under instructions from Nehru. However, as his sons from Saraswati—Gun Nidhi and Vidya Nidhi—were still studying he had no choice but to carry on managing the various cases. He entrusted the responsibility of liaising with government agencies and tax authorities to Vidya Nidhi and Gun Nidhi—once they joined the business, but kept the key decisions to be made with himself.

On his part, Ramkrishna focused on the businesses that remained operational. He frequently travelled to Dadri to visit the Dalmia Cement plant, to Rajpura for the biscuit factory, and to Ghaziabad for the Bhagwati Glass Works. The Keventers factory at Malcha Marg in Delhi also required his attention. Much of his work, however, was conducted from his home at Akbar Road.

After his jail term, Ramkrishna spent the rest of his years with Saraswati and their children at the Akbar Road house. He met his other wives and children occasionally or when protocol required it. Otherwise, he was content to spend his time with Saraswati and the seven children he had with her. His daily routine remained largely unchanged. Each morning, he went for his walk, followed by his customary massage.

After his morning routine, Ramkrishna would meet company executives at home. They discussed important business matters, and Ramkrishna would issue instructions that were then carried out. In the 1960s, Gun Nidhi and Vidya Nidhi had yet to join the business, leaving Ramkrishna and his trusted managers to oversee operations. A family loyalist, Rajeshwar, gradually took charge of all business affairs under Ramkrishna's supervision.

Ramkrishna would eat his food promptly at 7 p.m. every evening. He would go to the kitchen and sit cross-legged on the floor for his meal, insisting that all his children ate with him in the same manner. The children, still teenagers or younger, were not particularly fond of eating early or sitting cross-legged on the kitchen floor, but Ramkrishna's instructions had to be followed.

Soon after his elder son Gun Nidhi joined the business in 1970, Ramkrishna experienced a health scare. Despite his highly restricted diet, he developed high cholesterol. In 1972, he suffered a minor stroke but recovered quickly and well. Although he had to take some health precautions, his daily life remained largely unchanged.

By 1974, his son Vidya Nidhi had joined him in the business, allowing Ramkrishna to spend less time looking after business affairs and more time looking after the affairs of the soul. He immersed himself in religious discourses, conducted havans at home and wrote down his thoughts about life in general and his own journey in particular.

In 1977, Ramkrishna suffered a major stroke. This time, his recovery was neither quick nor easy. The stroke left him largely incapacitated. He was confined to bed and unable to lead the active life he once did.

However, Ramkrishna's mind remained sharp and needed constant engagement. Since he could no longer write as much as he once did, he relied on Saraswati and Vidya Nidhi to read to him. Saraswati would spend hours reading religious texts to him, while Vidya Nidhi would read out whatever Ramkrishna desired. Afterwards, Ramkrishna would insist on discussing the passages at length. At the time, the young man did not consider this the best use of his time, but in later years, he was grateful to his father for the grounding he had provided in all important matters.

Ramkrishna was largely at peace, but one fact gnawed at him constantly, especially after his stroke in 1977. The partition of the business and the manner in which he had lost his prized Times of India Group continued to haunt him.

He spoke about it to some of his close friends.

'After the departure of my able and trusted lieutenants—my brother and son-in-law—there was no one old enough in my immediate family to take their place full time. None of my sons were old enough. So, I worked alone. If even one son had been old enough to work with me by my side, things would have been very different today,' Ramkrishna would tell anyone who came to visit him.

Death had fascinated Ramkrishna throughout his life. Although he did not fear it, it did preoccupy his thoughts. His religious beliefs and extensive deliberations on its fundamental postulates had prepared him well for its inevitability. His main concern was that he did not know when it would strike him. He wanted to complete his life's work and settle his spiritual debts before leaving this world. His deepest desire was to free himself from the cycle of birth and rebirth.

'Whenever you confront death, don't waste your time in pity. Remind yourself, the very same thing will happen to you, and you do not know when. Every time someone dies, use it to reflect on your own mortality,' he would advise his children as he lay in bed.

Ramkrishna wanted his wives and children to be prepared for death. This meant they had to work as quickly as possible, accomplish as much as they could, and leave as little undone as possible. This, he said, needed to be kept in mind because of the uncertainty of life and the fact that death could strike at any time.

In spite of this awareness, Ramkrishna's spirit remained robust.

'There is nothing wrong with me. God had granted me a temporary respite to gather all my mental and physical resources. Do not worry, I will live for a hundred years,' he told one of his children as she looked down at him lying in bed.

Ramkrishna was in his eighties and quite ill during the last eighteen months of his life. Yet, he remained full of life. The moment a visitor entered his room, his face would light up, and he would immediately ask them to tell him something new. Jaidayal came to wish his elder brother every morning on his way to work. This would inevitably lead to a discussion on a number of topics. Ramkrishna's razor-sharp memory remained intact despite his ill health. One day, Shanti Prasad came to visit him along with his elder son Samir Jain. When he heard that Samir had been given the responsibility of Rohtas in Dalmianagar, Ramkrishna got agitated. He told Shanti Prasad not to waste Samir's talent in a loss making venture. Ramkrishna believed that Samir was sharp and intelligent and was meant for bigger things in life and business. It was after this that Samir Jain was assigned to the Times of India Group.

A day before his death, when the attending doctor asked him how he was feeling, Ramkrishna as usual, replied with folded hands and a smile on his face that he was perfectly all right.

Yet, his failing health could not be sustained by his optimistic spirit.

He died in the early hours of the morning of 26 September 1978, before dawn could break. It was, perhaps, the time he would have chosen for his death.

When he died, there was a peaceful smile on his face.

As the news of Ramkrishna's death spread, a crowd began gathering at the Akbar Road house. His other wives and their children were informed about the passing of the patriarch.

Saraswati had to make a decision regarding the cremation rites. Even though Asha Devi's son was Ramkrishna's eldest by birth, Saraswati knew that her husband had always looked upon Jaidayal as his son. In that sense, Jaidayal was the eldest son of the patriarch. Saraswati made the decision and requested her brother-in-law to lead the cremation rites at the crematorium.

As the sun began its descent in the west, Jaidayal lit the funeral pyre. The fading rays of the sun were met by the bright flames of the pyre. The family stood together, their arms around each other, watching as an era came to an end.

About the Series: Entrepreneurs Who Built India

*R*AMKRISHNA *Dalmia: The Fearless Risk-Taker* is the third book in the series Entrepreneurs Who Built India. The first two books of the series are *Gujarmal Modi: The Resolute Industrialist* and *Lala Shri Ram: The Man Who Saw Tomorrow.*

The second book of the series, *Lala Shri Ram*, has been awarded the prestigious Gaja Capital Business Book Prize 2024.

India has always been a land of entrepreneurs and businessmen. In fact, of the four varnas in our ancient caste system, the businessman/trader/merchant is one of them. The earliest records available show that the businessmen have played an important part in the country's economy at every stage.

About the Series: Entrepreneurs Who Built India

While businessmen have managed to flourish in every era, the time between 1947 and 1991 was perhaps the most challenging one for them. India became independent in 1947 and the newfound freedom brought forth aspirations and dreams for not just individual people but also collective dreams of social, political and economic freedom. However, the first Prime Minister envisaged a developmental model that had the state playing a dominant role as an entrepreneur as well as the funder of private businesses. The dreams of freedom that businessmen dreamt of in the new India quickly withered away as the British Raj was quickly replaced by the Licence Raj.

Due to the restrictions placed by the Licence Raj, which many say was a complex and opaque system, being an entrepreneur in India was a big headache. Further, the entrepreneurial spirit was kept in a tight leash by the complex system. Businesses were successful not so much because of what they did but because of who they knew. Such was the dependence on the benign hand of the government that businessmen, due to their association with the politician and bureaucrat, also were enveloped in the cloud of corruption in the minds of the general public.

However, people forget that there were many businesses, and indeed businessmen, during those very challenging times that worked tirelessly to make the new India. It certainly was not easy, but these businessmen persevered. True, they did learn how to 'manage' the system, but it did require entrepreneurial skills to set up, manage and grow the business within the tight framework of the system. Manufacturing is never an easy business and the Licence Raj made it even more difficult with the restrictions on the numbers to be produced. It is to the credit of the entrepreneurs of that era that they not only went about their work but also created products that became household names at that time.

Unfortunately, a large number of the businesses that were successful during the 1947–91 era are not visible today. The Gujar Mal Modi Group, the Shriram Group, the Dalmia Group, the Mafatlal Group, the Kamani Group are just a few names that were riding the success wave during the Licence Raj days but are present in a highly diluted manner or are almost forgotten today.

However, what cannot and should not be forgotten is their contribution to laying the foundation of the Indian economy and industry. If it were not for those stalwarts who worked against the odds and set up businesses, provided employment to many people and kept the Indian economy growing, the India of today would not be where she is currently. Thus, it is important to bring them out of their obscurity and present them to the new generation as the entrepreneurs who made India.

The book series Entrepreneurs Who Built India does just this. Each book in the series takes up a selected businessman (sadly, they were all men in those days with no woman business leader!) and his businesses. The stories provide to the reader a behind-the-scenes look into his life and business. Each book explores how he worked within the system to set up factories and other units to produce goods that India needed. The stories also bring out the challenges faced by them and the failures and successes in their businesses.

Each story brings into focus the dark shadow cast by the Licence Raj when, it was said, that one needed a licence just to breathe. The suffering that each businessman went through to run his business is highlighted, as is the grit and the determination that each one of them exhibited to never give in or give up. Besides these external factors, the story also highlights the aspects of entrepreneurship that the individual businessman exhibited. This was also an era when most of the businessmen did not have an MBA degree to their name. Thus, the inherent 'Indian Business Sense' is also be explored as each story is told. Further, the stories focus on success and the parameters of success. All in all, each story enables the reader to understand better what made the businessmen succeed in those years and to better appreciate the challenges they had to overcome to succeed.

As was said earlier, many of the successful businessmen of the 1947–91 era are no longer visible in the Indian corporate sector. Some preliminary research shows that businesses, and businessmen, who failed to adapt to the new environment post liberalization faded away quickly. A change in the external environment, over which they had no control, and the failure to adapt led to businesses going under. This becomes relevant in the current times. The coronavirus unleashed an unprecedented set of challenges for all businesses around the world at the same time. Businesses that have failed to adapt find themselves withering away in the post-Covid world. The series brings out the necessity for businesses to adapt to the changing external environment and provides lessons for readers as well.

Acknowledgements

AS always, I start by acknowledging my family—Juggi Bhasin, my husband, and Karan Bhasin, my son. I have said this earlier and say it again: these two men in my life are my anchors in the choppy seas of life. Between the last book and this one, I have gained a new member in my family. My daughter-in-law, Kshamta, who gives me the joy that only a daughter can.

I write about family businesses and, in that spirit, I must say that I am delighted to be part of the HarperCollins family! It has been a pleasure to work with Sachin Sharma, Publisher at HarperCollins Publishers. He has provided valuable inputs in his usual quiet and unassuming manner. But, as I have discovered, behind that calm exterior lies a very active and sharp mind! It is that mind that has provided the insightful guidance and unwavering support. Thank you, Sachin, for your constant support and guidance.

Shreya Lall, with her copyediting skills, sharpened the narrative. Her meticulous attention to detail and commitment to clarity have ensured that the narrative is tight and precise. Thank you, Shreya, for your inputs.

The first impression for a book is by its cover. Veer Mishra, the graphic designer, has delivered a stunning cover. Thank you, Veer.

The rest of the team at HarperCollins may have worked behind the scenes but their contribution is evident in the presentation of this book. Thank you, Team HarperCollins.

The book is about Ramkrishna Dalmia, and I had the privilege to spend time with three of his children—Gun Nidhi, Vidya Nidhi and Vasudha Dalmia.

Interacting with them and listening to them tell stories about their father, it was easy to sense the love, affection and respect they all had for him. It was also evident that the legacy of Ramkrishna Dalmia is being taken forward by them in their own way. Thank you, Gun Nidhi, V.N. and Vasudha, for your time and commitment towards this book.

My acknowledgements cannot be complete without thanking yet another family of mine—the family of my readers. Thank you, dear readers, for your comments, feedback and suggestions. Do keep them coming as any interaction with you truly encourages me further.

References

'Plague in India', 16 November 2017, https://www.thehindu.com/archives/plague-in-india/article20461152.ece

Agico Cement, 'All about the Wet Process of Cement Manufacturing', https://www.cementplantequipment.com/all-about-the-wet-process-of-cement-manufacturing/

Anurag Singhal, 'How luck played a major role in success of Ramkrishna Dalmia, The Marwaris', https://www.youtube.com/watch?v=czBqoqgPmSg

Bagalkot Cement, 'History of Indian cement industry', https://www.linkedin.com/pulse/history-indian-cement-industry-bagalkot-cement/

Balachandran, Manu, 'An Indian Irish billionaire's journey from outsider to kingmaker and then opponent at the Tata Group', https://scroll.in/article/820018/an-indian-irish-billionaires-journey-from-outsider-to-kingmaker-and-then-opponent-at-the-tata-group

Bhandari, Bhupesh, 'How politicians should deal with businessmen', 3 December 2010, https://www.rediff.com/money/column/guest-how-politicians-should-deal-with-businessmen/20101203.htm

Bhandari, Bhupesh, 'Little black books', 20 January 2013, https://www.business-standard.com/article/beyond-business/little-black-books-110022000016_1.html

Bose, Sajal, 'Dalmia Cement: Making a mark', https://businessindia.co/magazine/dalmia-cement-making-a-mark

Business Line, 'The Marwari business model-II', 8 April 2013, https://www.thehindubusinessline.com/opinion/columns/harish-damodaran/the-marwari-business-model-ii/article64540109.ece

Chopra, P.N., *Quit India Movement II – Role of Indian Big Business*, South Asia Books, 1992.

Daily Motion, The Rise and Fall of R.K. Dalmia as a Pioneer of Business', https://www.dailymotion.com/video/x88aedx

Dalmia, Seth Ramkrishna, *A short sketch of the beginning of my life, and a guide to bliss*.

Dalmia, Vidya Nidhi, 'Opposites Attract', *Hindustan Times*, 14 November 2007.

Dalmia, Vidya Nidhi, 'Opposites attract', *Hindustan Times*, https://www.hindustantimes.com/india/opposites-attract/story-wXJMeZ9nWqBg8dAV5iz7fP.html

Damodaran, Harish, '7 decades before Hindenburg-Adani, a speech by Feroze Gandhi that sank a business house', Indian Express, 14 February 2023, https://indianexpress.com/article/

opinion/columns/7-decades-ago-a-speech-that-sank-a-corporate-8439381/

Deo, Saudamini, 'Dineshnandini: The writer who lost more from love and life than she gained from literature', 28 April 2019, https://scroll.in/article/919788/dineshnandini-the-writer-who-lost-more-from-love-and-life-than-she-gained-from-literature

Desai, Hari, 'Dalmia: A Romantic Industrialist closed to Jinnah', 17 June 2020, https://www.asian-voice.com/Opinion/Columnists/Hari-Desai/Dalmia-A-Romantic-Industrialist-closed-to-Jinnah

Enotes, 'How did stock brokers earn money from stock sales in the 1920s?', https://www.enotes.com/topics/history/questions/20s-how-did-stockbrocker-earn-money-sale-stock-253813

Harishankar Dwedi and Jaidayal Dalmia (eds), *Karmyogi Shri Ramkrishna Dalmia: Smritigranth, part one*.

Hazari, R.K. *The Structure of the Corporate Private Sector*, Planning Commission, 1966.

Index Daily, 'From Stealing Jewellery to One of India's Richest', https://www.instagram.com/index.daily/p/CdaTHqSlNQf/?img_index=7

India Kanoon, 'R. K. Dalmia vs Delhi Administration on 5 April 1962', https://indiankanoon.org/doc/434894/

Indian Numismatics, 'Table of Eras', https://www.indiannumismatics.com/table-of-eras.php

Investopedia, 'CSE', https://www.investopedia.com/terms/c/cse.asp

Investopedia, 'Syndicate: Definition, How It Works, and Types of Syndicate', https://www.investopedia.com/terms/s/syndicate.asp

Investopedia, 'The Art of Speculation', https://www.investopedia.com/articles/basics/12/art-of-speculation.asp

Kallury, Kruttika, 'Family Matters', India Today, 7 April 2011, http://indiatoday.intoday.in/story/family-matters/1/134585.html.

Manmohan, Nutan, 'RK Dalmia's empire was next only to Tata, Birla. But his tryst with news proved costly', 15 April 2023, https://theprint.in/feature/rk-dalmias-empire-was-next-only-to-tata-birla-but-his-tryst-with-news-proved-costly/1520021/

Marwar India Magazine, 'The Rags to Riches Story of Ramkrishna Dalmia', https://www.marwar.com/archive/the-rags-to-riches-story-of-ramkrishna-dalmia/

Marwar India Magazine, 'The Sahu Jains of Najibabad', https://www.marwar.com/archive/the-sahu-jains-of-najibabad/#:~:text=Sahu%20Salek%20Chand%20had%20three,was%20Rai%20Bahadur%20Jagmandar%20Das.

Mehrotra, Anandita, 'Dinesh Nandini Dalmia — Nehru's 'mysterious one', a Hindi writer and a feminist icon', The Print, 16 February 2022, https://theprint.in/theprint-profile/dinesh-nandini-dalmia-nehrus-mysterious-one-a-hindi-writer-and-a-feminist-icon/833418/

Menon Malhan, Sangita P. *The TOI Story: How a Newspaper Changed the Rules of the Game.* HarperCollins, 2013.

Mitra, Sumit, 'Court cases become only occasion for Dalmia family reunion', 15 October 1980, https://www.

indiatoday.in/magazine/economy/story/19801015-court-cases-become-only-occasion-for-dalmia-family-reunion-821492-2014-01-06

Newshour, 'Success story of a tycoon with a mission', https://www.newshour.press/news-hour-special/success-story-tycoons-mission/

Organiser, 'Jinnah's Air India shares and his lavish mansions', https://organiser.org/2013/08/25/111709/bharat/jinnah-s-air-india-shares-and-his-lavish-mansions/

Patherya, Mudar, 'If you knew Calcutta the way I know Calcutta', https://www.telegraphindia.com/my-kolkata/places/if-you-knew-calcutta-the-way-i-know-calcutta/cid/1978097

Press Reader, 'Gandhi's coterie did not let Dalmia prevail over Jinnah on Partition', https://www.pressreader.com/india/the-sunday-guardian/20150621/281921656685160

Ramkrishna Dalmia: An indomitable spirit', 16 August 2008, https://www.ndtv.com/video/shows/india-inc/ramkrishna-dalmia-an-indomitable-spirit-37160

Ramkrishna Dalmia: The Great Visionary, *Sunday Mail Special Feature*, 19-25 April 1992.

Roy, Shubhrangshu, The lives and wives of R.K. Dalmia, *Economic Times*.

Rozario, Jospeh. The rags-to-riches story of Ramkrisna Dalmia, Marwar India, https://www.marwar.com/the-rags-to-riches-story-of-ramkrishna-dalmia/

Sagarmal Sharma, *Chirawa – Ateet Se Aaj Tak*.

Sharma, Sagar Mal, *Chirawa Ka Itihas*, Chirawa Shodh Sansthan, 1990.

Srivastava, Sanjay, 'Pocket was empty, Pandit looked at Dalmia's hand and said- luck will change in a week', News 18, https://hindi.news18.com/news/knowledge/once-india-richest-person-rk-dalmia-who-change-his-fortune-self-and-great-friend-of-jinnah-3550508.html

Stories Indica, 'From Stealing Wife's Jewellery To One of India's Richest', https://storiesindica.substack.com/p/from-stealing-wifes-jewellery-to

Subramanian, N. Sundaresha, 'Ramkrishna Dalmia first spoke out against cow slaughter', https://www.business-standard.com/article/beyond-business/first-spoke-out-against-cow-slaughter-115042400925_1.html

Tandon, Prakash, *Banking century: A short history of banking in India and the pioneer: Punjab National Bank* Penguin, 1989.

Tata, 'Sir Nowroji Saklatvala', https://www.tata.com/about-us/tata-group-our-heritage/tata-titans/sir-nowroji-saklatvala

The better India, 'Icmic, Santosh & Rukmani: The Forgotten Story of India's Original Cookers', https://www.thebetterindia.com/232537/first-pressure-cooker-make-in-india-santosh-icmic-rukmani-prestige-hawkins-iconic-brand-history/

Timberg, Thomas A. *The Marwaris: From Jagat Seth to the Birlas*. Penguin Books, 2014.

TIME, 'India: Fadeout', https://time.com/archive/6870309/india-fadeout/

Udaipur Blog, 'Dinesh Nandini Dalmia: People from Udaipur you should know about', https://udaipurblog.com/dinesh-nandini-dalmia.html

Wikipedia, 'Chirawa', https://en.wikipedia.org/wiki/Chirawa

Wikipedia, '1934 Indian General Election', https://en.wikipedia.org/wiki/1934_Indian_general_election

Wikipedia, 'Dalmia Group', https://en.wikipedia.org/wiki/Dalmia_Group#:~:text=On%2031%20May%201948%2C%20the,legal%20document%20to%20this%20effect.

Wikipedia, 'The Times of India', https://en.wikipedia.org/wiki/The_Times_of_India

Wikipedia, ACC, https://en.wikipedia.org/wiki/ACC_(company)

Wikipedia, Dalmia Group, https://en.wikipedia.org/wiki/Dalmia_Group

World Retain Congress 2025, http://www.technopak.com/Files/qsr-market-in-india.pdf

Yogapedia, 'Sandhya Kala', 21 December 2023, https://www.yogapedia.com/definition/11265/sandhya-kala

Other sources

Autobiographies by Ramkrishna Dalmia, 1962 and 1973, self-published.

Dalmia Bharat Silver Jubilee Souvenir, brought out by Dalmia Bharat Cement company, a private publication.

Dalmia family tree, provided by Vidya Nidhi Dalmia, Ramkrishna Dalmia's son.

Meera Chatterjee's autobiography, self-published.

Pamphlets by Ramkrishna Dalmia.

TOI News Items Digital Collection, archival digitized material from the Times of India archives.

HarperCollins *Publishers* India

At HarperCollins India, we believe in telling the best stories and finding the widest readership for our books in every format possible. We started publishing in 1992; a great deal has changed since then, but what has remained constant is the passion with which our authors write their books, the love with which readers receive them, and the sheer joy and excitement that we as publishers feel in being a part of the publishing process.

Over the years, we've had the pleasure of publishing some of the finest writing from the subcontinent and around the world, including several award-winning titles and some of the biggest bestsellers in India's publishing history. But nothing has meant more to us than the fact that millions of people have read the books we published, and that somewhere, a book of ours might have made a difference.

As we look to the future, we go back to that one word—a word which has been a driving force for us all these years.

Read.